SURVIVING MADMEN

One Woman's Encounters with a Governor,

Two Congressmen, and a Spouse

JERRI LYNN SPARKS

Black Rose Writing | Texas

First printing

Some names and identifying details may have been changed to protect the privacy of individuals.

ISBN: 978-1-68433-191-8
PUBLISHED BY BLACK ROSE WRITING
www.blackrosewriting.com

Printed in the United States of America
Suggested Retail Price (SRP) $16.95

Surviving Madmen is printed in Garamond

For my children. Love wins. Love always wins.

SURVIVING
MADMEN

CHAPTER 1:
"PROVE TO ME YOU'RE A WOMAN"

"We are not here to curse the darkness, but to light the candle that can guide us through that darkness to a safe and sane future." — John F. Kennedy

On July 5, 2012, I nearly died...I was lying on the cold tile floor of my home's guest room at 3:00 a.m., half-naked and terrified. An angry, deranged man's hands were tightly wrapped around my throat trying to choke the life out of me. I couldn't scream for help, his grip was too tight, his determination too focused on ending me.

"Seven of my friends told me you are a man!" he had screamed through the locked guest room door an hour earlier as he paced back and forth. I could see him through the beveled glass that made up the top half of the door of the guest room which used to serve as an examining room when the old 1906-era home had served double duty as a doctor's home and medical office. The hall light was on and faint light filtered into the room I was now trapped in.

"Come out here and prove to me you're a woman!" he had demanded. I could barely make out his shape through the glass, but it looked as if he was still angrily pacing back and forth past the door as if he was trying to decide on his next actions.

Alarmed and panicked, I had quietly scrambled around the room on my hands and knees in the dark looking for a way out. The windows in the 106-year-old house were sealed tight from layers of paint and nails as if someone had purposely boarded them up. I had only recently moved into the guest room and hadn't thought to check the windows to see if they would open when I had moved into the room seven months earlier because I had done so in mid-December when it was very cold out in western New York. Now it was early July.

I picked up my cell phone and quickly dialed 9-1-1 but hesitated to press "send" because for two weeks the man had been saying "The first cop dies" if I tried to call for help. I knew that by the time the police arrived (at least ten minutes by my estimation) I would be long dead and possibly my children would be dead too.

So I kept the phone in my hand, primed to hit "send" on the 9-1-1 call I'd plugged in and begun reaching under the guest bed for something to fight back with. I also kept telling myself that he would never hurt me because he had never tried to do so before, not really…Still, I was scared, so I tried to find anything to help me should the unthinkable happen.

Suddenly, my hands felt a long cardboard box. I pulled it out and could see it was a pellet gun still in its factory box, a gift that had been given to me for Christmas by a friend I'd met who was a hunter. I had no pellets in the house for the air rifle (I stored them in a separate place), but maybe I could fool him with it or use it like a baseball bat. I kept going over to the bookshelf searching for anything else I could use to defend myself, but there was nothing in the room except for books. I told myself if necessary I could lob "Great Expectations" at his head and hope for a Dickensian rescue story but most of the books in the guest room were small paperbacks. The heavy academic hardcovers were in the built-in shelves in the living room down the long hallway, and I couldn't get to them.

I walked over to the two windows and again tried to pry one of them open. One of them had an air conditioner in it but it was too heavy and noisy for me to move without it crashing and breaking, therefore alerting him that I was trying to escape out the window. It was dark out and the courtyard beyond the guest room had a ten-foot cinderblock wall encircling it that blocked the neighbor's view into the room. I was essentially a sitting duck.

The sad realization of being trapped began to sink in. It was around 2:30 a.m. and I had no family in the state. My exit routes were blocked and I had a six-foot-two, two hundred-and-fifty-pound angry spouse on the other side of a half glass door. If ever I felt like a damsel in distress, this was it. Only I had no knight in shining armor to save me. Some fairy tale I was living.

Meanwhile, this crazy man was pacing back and forth in the hallway, whose bright light he had turned on an hour earlier making him seem more sharp and frightening. I could see his blurry outline and he appeared to have no shirt on. He was a pale man of Norwegian and German descent who could not really tan so his skin reflected off the light. He was overweight but surprisingly strong and quick. His longish, graying wavy hair was flying unkempt around his head like it was alive and he was breathing very heavily. He reminded me of a gorilla I'd once seen at the zoo who was upset about his food being stolen.

I was terrified. No longer did he resemble the kind and educated, happy and success-destined man I had married with so much hope twenty years earlier. He was now a frothing, angry shell of what I used to think of as my best friend. I was suddenly in the presence of a madman.

"Do you want a divorce!?" he had yelled from the hallway. By this time I knew I had no way out of the room or the house. If I said "yes" to wanting a divorce he would expect me to open the door to talk but I knew he would try to force me to have sex with him if I got anywhere near him, something he had asked for around 10:30 p.m. the night before, July 4th, 2012, when our argument had first begun in this latest round of arguments.

There was no way I was having sex with him. I had truly rather die than allow him to touch me ever again. The last time we had actually been intimate was a long time before this night and I remember afterwards going to shower and just crying, feeling like I couldn't wash myself hard enough to get the residue of him off of me. I vowed to myself in the shower that day "Never again. That is the last time."

And it was. I kept that promise to myself. He had become a horrible husband and a rapidly deteriorating father and I wanted out. But every time I tried to discuss ending the marriage maturely it devolved into threats.

"I'll take the kids and the house is mine," he would growl at me. I didn't know it at the time but he had somehow manipulated my name off of the house so that only my name was on the deed. I remembered signing papers when we bought the house so I don't know how he accomplished this. I've never found out. His mother knew this though because when we first started having marital problems after our move from California to New York so he could become a university psychology professor, something I had encouraged him to do to earn a steady income for a change, she noticed on some real estate paperwork that my name wasn't on the loan papers. While she didn't tell me this, she did insist that we all go to the local agent and put my name on the deed to the house complete with a notary public.

At the time I'd just had a baby so my mind was preoccupied with infant care, older child care and keeping our young son with autism safe. I was overwhelmed with three kids in diapers, the oldest of whom was disabled, nursing my infant and trying to run a house. Real estate transactions were the farthest thing from my mind. Besides, I trusted my husband. We had three kids together, why would I be suspicious of our home loan papers?

I remember my husband being annoyed with his mother when she insisted on this transaction but he deferred to his mother's insistence and we completed the deed paperwork with a notary public. I now wonder if she knew something I didn't know about his plans and was helping to keep my interests safe. Whatever her reasoning, it did protect me financially and I'm forever grateful for that at least.

When I had said "no" about having sex with my husband earlier that night on July 4th, 2012, I had reminded him that we hadn't been getting along for over a year and I was not going to have sex with him. He had treated me terribly, cheated on me and was verbally abusing us all. This was hardly the environment for sex, I had said.

Enraged, he had sprung straight up from the bed and growled at me "You better watch it!" and then he'd stormed out of the guest room.

Obviously, I was afraid but by this time he had been threatening me for at least a year and then he'd resort to apologizing. I had been a stay-at-home mom for around eight years caring for my disabled son and I didn't have a job or means of supporting myself. My disabled son took all of my time and energy. We also lived in New York with no family in the state and my family lived all the way in North Carolina.

Instead of divorcing, we had gone to marital counseling many times. It always worked for a while and then the same behaviors would slowly creep back in. I wanted to work to find a way out of this dying marriage but after being out of the job market for so long it was going to take some rebuilding, which was difficult with a disabled son and three other young children at home by this time. He had wanted me to have a fifth child and I absolutely refused and took measures to ensure I would not be having any more children, which disappointed him. I thought he was insane just for wanting another child after all we were dealing with.

After he had threatened me for refusing to have sex with him, I had tiptoed to the guest room door and locked it, thinking that was it. The deadbolt was engaged and a second flap lock was folded across the door seal. I thought I was safe and that he was going to cool down and go sulk in the basement watching some movies in his "workshop." He was a media addict and spent an inordinate amount of time in fantasy, watching fiction shows in the basement while the rest of the family slept, reading fiction as opposed to biography most of the time, and from what I could tell, living fiction. He even had an Master's in Fine Arts in Creative Writing from the best writer's program in the country, the prestigious Iowa Writer's Workshop at the University of Iowa.

I had to go to work early the next morning at my new job, and I didn't want to be late so I tried to convince myself that all was fine. This was just another mini-argument. I'd gotten quite used to the sporadic outbursts from my spouse, and I had a high tolerance for chaos, my mind being slowly conditioned over time to deal with sudden stressors that come with the raising of an autistic child who regularly melted down and escaped back then.

Around 1:30 a.m. he had flipped on the hall light, which woke me up and then he inexplicably left the house. Confused and still not realizing the dangerous situation I was dealing with, I called him on his cell phone and asked him what he was doing. I said "I have to be at work at 8AM tomorrow and I need you to watch the kids. Where are you going at this time of the morning? I need you to come back home and go to sleep so the kids will be okay while I'm at work."

This was a huge mistake.

Who knows where he was going? I never found out. If I had just let him go off in his car at 1:30 a.m., maybe none of what happened next would have happened. So many times I've replayed this scenario in my mind, sometimes it will just come out of nowhere when I'm going to sleep. I wonder if I hadn't called him back if I wouldn't have gotten hurt. Would we have been able to have an amicable divorce? Or was he going to make things even worse?

But it did happen...so I did what he had earlier demanded – I proved to him I was most definitely a woman. As William Congreve's line from the play 'The Mourning Bride' implies, "Hell hath no fury like a woman scorned."

CHAPTER 2:
KEEPING EVERYTHING

Around 2:30 a.m. I heard the mudroom doors unlocking, first the outer one and then the second one at the top of the stairs. Both doors have small rectangular glass panels so they were quite noisy when opened. Then I heard his heavy footsteps returning to our home. He shut the mudroom doors and locked them. I could hear the chain of the deadbolt latch on the top and third lock on the inner door. He and I had both gotten so used to locking our home like it was Fort Knox because of our son with autism's tendency to run away any chance he could get. It had made me filled with what is now acknowledged to be Post-Traumatic Stress Syndrome in the caregivers of young children with autism due to their erratic behaviors and unsafe tendencies. So we lived as if we were in a fortress and had a lock on every door and window and an alarm on most of them. The very things I had used to keep my son safe were now causing me to be unsafe.

My husband was big and imposing, six feet and two inches tall and he weighed around two hundred and fifty pounds. He had struggled most of his adulthood with weight problems, something that had surprised me because he had been very thin when we were dating and when we first got married. But after the wedding, I noticed he had slowly begun to change in several ways and not just physically.

He got moody and had odd sleeping patterns. He would insist we walk to UCLA campus around 10 PM and stay there working and kidding around the empty campus until daylight the next morning. While those were fun and memorable experiences that seemed to belong in a John Hughes movie (once we took a wheeled office chair and he zoomed me up and down the hallways avoiding the janitors, another time we snuck up to the rooftop of Franz Hall and looked down at the darkened campus as if it was our own private terrace up there), we were both older now and I was ready to be more serious in life. I wanted to have normal sleep and waking hours so I could finish my degree and hold down a steady job.

The transition to adulthood and normalcy was hard for him though. Even though he was five years older than me, he was much more immature. He seemed to need a Bohemian lifestyle that was incongruent with my steady goals.

He obtained his Ph.D. in Cognitive Neuroscience, but then he refused to look for work and chose instead to lie on the couch all day watching TV or playing the interactive video game "Doom" with a friend, completely ignoring me and his personal hygiene for nine solid months. I asked him why he wasn't applying for jobs like all his friends were and he said: "They will come to me."

They never came to him.

I had to push him to apply for work. I had to push him to wake up and shower. I tried to get him to see a counselor but he was angry at me for suggesting he needed help. He of all people would recognize if he needed help since he'd just gotten his Ph.D. in Cognitive Neuroscience from one of the top brain research schools in the country he had said on many occasions. He was fine and the jobs would come to him.

Somehow he had thought that the world was just waiting for his greatness and would recognize it and lavish him with job offers once he became a doctor. How could such an intellectually gifted person think like this? It was mesmerizing to watch but frustrating to live with. When nothing materialized he fell into an even deeper, darker place.

After nearly a year of being ignored and after trying everything I could to reach him, I left. I moved out and got my own place in Santa Monica. It was a scary move for me because he was the only person I really knew in California. Sure, I had work colleagues and some college laboratory friends but I didn't know them that well at the time. I had no family in the state and very little money. (The pattern of isolating me from my family had begun before we were even married but I didn't recognize it at the time so early on in our relationship.) I was twenty-four and all alone in the big city of Los Angeles, California, one of the world's biggest economies and also one of the most expensive and busiest and noisiest places to live.

Still, I made a go of it. I kept busy and took on extra work editing manuscripts for professors who studied hostile masculinity (how's that for irony?). I ate lots of canned food and borrowed friends' furniture just to have a place to sleep and a table and chairs to eat dinner on in my one-room studio apartment that was right beside the freeway. It was noisy but it was mine.

I lost a lot of weight that I didn't need to lose to begin with so that I looked way too skinny. The nights alone in my noisy freeway-hugging apartment were awful. I didn't sleep so much as stare out the window until I noticed a pair of feet right under the curtains. The neighbor's son had begun smoking cigarettes by my bedside window which frightened me since he was mere inches away from my bed just outside the window. When I had moved in my friend Mick and I had left my mattress and TV outside the apartment to go get another load from the car and in those few minutes it took to walk down two flights of stairs to the curb, my mattress and TV had been stolen. So it's not outside of reason for me to have been afraid of the neighbor smoking right outside my window at 2:00 a.m.

This half-alive lifestyle lasted about three months before my husband and I worked things out and decided to give our marriage another try. Our parents had pushed us hard to try to reconcile and I finally relented. We didn't have kids yet and I had seen the messed up dating pool in Los Angeles and thought maybe I should try things again with my husband. After all, the devil you know is safer than the devil you don't know, right?

It remains a decision I sometimes re-examine when life is hard and I'm stressed. I love where I've ended up in life but I had to go through some actual Hell to get here.

Once we got back together, sometimes my spouse would dress very nicely, other times he looked like a homeless man, especially the last few years of our marriage. As a result, I was embarrassed by his appearance most of the last several years of our relationship. It was so bad that at parties people could not believe that we were a couple. I couldn't blame them because I couldn't believe it myself. A few folks even said to me

"How did *he* get *you?*" By this time he had worn down my confidence so much that I was surprised when they said that. I didn't realize my own worth in my early to mid-twenties. And by the time I did, I had four children with him and had much more at stake.

I was very busy raising our four children, the oldest of whom has autism and needs constant supervision, so I didn't have time to micromanage my spouse or devote a lot of time ruminating on the things I was unhappy about. I loved being a mother so I focused on that. I wrote articles about motherhood and autism in the local and national papers and even became the national science writer for the Autism Science Foundation to find meaning and to use my degree. My husband did not support me in any of these endeavors and even actively encouraged me not to do anything except be a stay-at-home mom. I resented his lack of support in my personal goals and his lack of helping me around the house. While he did some rudimentary things if I asked him to, he had no self-motivation to help out. He hired a lawn service for our half acre of land. He hired so many sitters to help watch the kids that I had to run their schedules like a home business. And we simply could not afford this "staff" that he insisted on. It got so bad between us that folks rarely ever saw us out together.

To make things worse, after our youngest child was born he admitted that he had an affair during the pregnancy and at that point I asked him for a divorce. Actually I demanded a divorce but I had no money to go through with it. I was still nursing our baby and had no job. He refused to grant me a cordial divorce and because I was a stay-at-home mom with no money or family nearby at the time, I agreed to once again go to counseling with him.

It was a waste of time. So…I made a promise to myself that I was getting out.

The very next day after that I began jogging. I sat in the rocking chair glider in my baby's room and consciously nursed him for the last time. He was two years old. It was time. I remember staring out the window of his pale-blue-painted room and crying silently as my baby nursed. The sweet happy life I thought my husband and I had rebuilt together was a sham. It was time for my happy and authentic reality.

So I put my two-year-old son in the stroller, bundled him up in a snowsuit and lots of blankets and a stroller shield and began jogging in the snow. This was late February and by April I was running 5K races. I went from a size 10 to a size 2 in just a few months and won my first race in my age group. My husband, of course, wasn't there to support me. He had gone to the race with me but snuck out to go see a tall blonde before I crossed the finish line. I won a steak dinner that day but I lost any hope of ever being appreciated by my husband. I needed a job and fast.

But finding a job after being a stay-at-home mom for eight years was tough. Time passed, and I kept building up my skills and raising my children but with the idea in mind that as soon as all the kids were in school full-time and I had a good paying job I was leaving him. During this time there were good times though, which made it easier to wait for the right moment. We essentially went through the motions, having emotional holidays where we glanced across the room at each other, proud of our little toddlers, to then having moments of complete hatred when he once again did nothing for my birthday and yet expected me to herald him from on high on his.

I had been wanting a divorce off and on for eight years due to his neglect of me and the children (yelling, refusing to find steady work, not helping around the house, extramarital affairs that I suspected but could not prove, completely forgetting my birthday or spending a lot of money on things that had no meaning at all to me, such as $100 in tabloid magazines for one birthday or $700 worth of maternity dresses in my last month of pregnancy "to make up for" never celebrating the birth of our children but instead going to the movies the day I brought the baby home from the hospital) and every time I almost had enough money to leave and support us, something would happen (either my son with autism would be hospitalized and I needed the parental support for the other younger children or my economic means of leaving would be lost when a job ended).

He also ate constantly or not at all. What he did eat was junk food and soda and beer. He fed our kids junk food and soda despite my admonitions to stop. I was living with a college frat boy! He would sleep all day and be awake all night, disrupting the normal flow of life in the house for me and the children. It was just like he was back in college with his nocturnal ways. It is very difficult to sleep when someone is listening to music all night long with the lights on, running up and down the stairs making noise. We had no normalcy. This was a sporadic spiral with him.

It reminded me of our early years together, a place I thought we had matured away from. I rarely saw him during our third year of marriage out in Los Angeles and after nine months of this I left him and got my own place. We didn't have children yet so I was trying to make a clean break. I was young, twenty-four or twenty-five years old, and he was about thirty. I said we could still be friends but that was all we should be. But over a few months' time he straightened his life back up and I believed it was for real. The man I had married returned so I went back to him. He was excellent at convincing people he had changed. In fact, he is just excellent at convincing people of anything, period, including doctors, therapists and law enforcement.

He never forgave me for leaving him in the third year of our marriage though. He held onto his resentment over our three-month separation for years and I had no idea...I had written off his sudden checking out of life after college as some sort of post-graduate school minor depression, not knowing his long and significant mental health history, something he and his family kept from me and which I wouldn't learn of until after we finally split for good when I went to our attic and found a box of medical records buried deep under some other papers. Everyone had kept this knowledge from me, even his college advisers, whom I knew well. At what point is there an obligation to warn someone about a potentially dangerous person you intend to marry and have children with?

When I saw the paperwork indicating the very serious mental condition he had been diagnosed with years before I even met him, my heart sank. I could have avoided all this hardship in life if someone, anyone, had been honest with me. They were trying to protect him, but no one was trying to protect me.

I also didn't know the depths of his anger and narcissism and how my leaving him in 1995 had wounded him and his very fragile ego. It had been an amicable split, or so I thought, complete with a cute conversation where we sat down in our Brentwood apartment, just two miles away from where O.J. Simpson had killed his ex-wife, Nicole Brown Simpson, only a year earlier in 1994, and methodically went through our possessions. I remember saying to him at the time of the O.J. Simpson arrest "You better not ever lay a hand on me and if you do, you better hit to kill because I will fight back." I now shudder over the prophetic nature of that statement. At the time when I said it, I was joking because it never occurred to me that my husband could ever try to hurt me. So when we were dividing up our marital possessions only three years after our marriage, we only had a minor disagreement over who got The Beatles' "White Album" and the Riverside Shakespeare. It was the most academic of splits.

Mutual friends remarked that it was the nicest parting they'd ever seen. One friend even remarked "Well, if you two can't make it there's no hope for marriage." We were that happy in our marriage at one point. It's hard to believe now that this was ever the case.

Our split was so amicable it gave us both pause. Were we making a mistake? I was nice so I let him have what he wanted and just took my things and got my own place in Santa Monica. We even hung out as friends after the split, going to the movies and talking on the phone and chatting at parties. We even shared custody of our cats. This went on for three months until he convinced me to take him back by being sweet and attentive and caring about his health and well-being. We had both dabbled in the dating pool and saw that what was out there was not that great and we were a known quantity to each other. I was also about childrearing age so I had that to consider as well. Being from the South where women tend to have babies early, I was already twenty-six years old and either going to get divorced or reconcile with my Ivy League-educated husband and start a family. So we got back together and immediately began trying to have children and I thought everything was fine. Crisis avoided.

But everything was not fine. Instead, his long-range plan to punish me was just beginning.

Little did I know he could hold a grudge for a very long time and he could plot with the best of the madmen, something I would find out the hard way many years later. When he had wanted to keep all the things years earlier, I had relented because it was just material things, but it was an ominous foreshadowing of how he would respond when I finally admitted I wanted a divorce once we had a house and children together. In his mind he would be losing everything and he couldn't allow that. One way or another he was going to keep everything...

On this particular night, July 4th, 2012, he again looked like a homeless man. His clothing was ripped and dirty, and his hair hadn't been cut in months. His shoes had holes in them which he sometimes patched together with duct tape instead of buying a new pair. His glasses had broken at the hinge, and instead of using my insurance to repair them, he had used wire to fuse them back together, something I'd learn up close and personal in a few hours.

I had money to buy new clothes for him but he kept choosing the raggedy items until I threw them away, a practice which enraged him. He had this dingy, yellow mustard colored sweatshirt that I had bought him in grad school that had so many stains and holes in it years later that I wouldn't be seen in public with him if he wore it. One day I tossed it out when I was doing the laundry because the holes were more prevalent than the intact material. Once he realized his raggedy and threadbare sweatshirt was gone he flipped out. The tantrum he threw over his missing sweatshirt was like something you'd see from a toddler.

So I bought him a new one similar to it and learned that "It just isn't 'golden boy.'" I ended up digging the old one out of the trash and giving it back to him, and he continued wearing it.

"Great," I thought. "So my grown spouse names his clothing." I have a great sense of humor so I tried to make it a humorous thing but after initially laughing with me, I could tell he was serious. I had committed an infringement on *his* property. I had no idea a person could be so attached to a raggedy sweatshirt.

I would learn later that he had incredible difficulty letting go of *anything*, including discarded household items, broken parts of furniture, wrappers, boxes, pets, and people. (He also saved receipts of all sorts so that when we finally did split, I found his "massage parlor" receipts from when he was supposed to be traveling to the west coast for a "conference.")

When we had moved into our house in September 2001, there was an old pool table in the basement that we decided not to keep. It took up most of the room where we wanted to give the kids a playroom to ride their tricycles indoors in the harsh Upstate New York winters, and I wanted to assemble their slide and playhouse in the space. So we dismantled the pool table and it was his job to throw out all the parts of the pressed wood and other useless parts. Our oldest child was three years old at the time so by the time he could even play pool, it would be years and years later. It made perfect sense to get rid of the pool table so the kids could spend their toddler and elementary years playing. After trying to sell the table with no takers, the vote was to tear it apart, at least that's what I thought.

Eleven years later in 2012 after he attacked me, I was clearing out the house and moving when I found the discarded pressed wood remnants of the pool table shoved in the corner of the unfinished side of the basement. It was destroyed so it had no chance of being reassembled and it was of no value. I have no idea why he saved it, but he never could make himself throw it away. He couldn't throw anything away.

He also hoarded strange supplies like hair conditioner (for the apocalypse?) and bar soap, items that aren't exactly survivalist in nature, instead of staple foods and water. I'd ask him why he kept buying conditioner and bar soap and he'd say "I got it for free with these coupon deals!" When I reminded him that we had enough conditioner to last years so he could stop now he would just look at me like I was killing his buzz. Going to the Dollar General store two or even three times a day for "deals" was his daily routine, along with several stops per day at the coffee shop. All our money went to wasteful junk and he never parted with anything. When his big screen TV finally died, it nearly killed him taking it to the curb so I ended up doing it myself. When our twelve-year-old cat was dying a three-year slow death by diabetes and it was finally time because the poor cat was suffering greatly after I gave him daily insulin injections for three years to the cost of $3,600, I was the one who had to make the call to the veterinarian's office. I was headed out the door with the cat before my husband stepped up to take him himself. He just could not part with things or creatures, even when those creatures are suffering.

He just wanted to keep everything – especially life as he had known it…

CHAPTER 3:
"I DIDN'T MEAN TO DO THAT"

As he made his way through the tile-floored mudroom and into the hallway near the guest room a little after 2AM on July 5th, 2012, I woke up. I still didn't realize how serious the situation was because he had never been physically abusive in a classical sense before, at least not what I recognized as physical abuse at the time.

It would only be after going through counseling that I would remember that during our first year of marriage twenty years earlier his car had broken down just off Sunset Boulevard in Brentwood near UCLA campus on his way home from work one evening and it had led to an incident between us. It was an old white Chevrolet Impala with at least 100,000 miles on it. His parents, whom I adored and who were very fine and upstanding, charitable folks living on Cape Cod, had given it to him as they had every car he had ever owned. (He was in his forties before he ever got a car in his own name and that was only because I made him buy a mini-van once our fourth child was born. I, on the other hand, got my first car all by myself when I was just nineteen years old with no co-signer and I paid it off as well and drove it for ten years until I moved back East after college. I also didn't get so attached to the car that I flipped out when I left it behind.)

The car was already on its last legs when his folks gave it to us. It was rusting and needed maintenance. Instead of caring for it, my husband drove that car like a tank in the military. So it was no surprise to me when its axle finally broke on Sunset Boulevard and Barrington Avenue as he was driving home one evening. He never could commit to maintenance to keep things working properly – not his vehicles, not his clothing, not his body nor his relationships. His previous car his parents had given him was a pea green Chevrolet Impala that was so worn out you could see through the floorboards, a very disturbing image to see the road flying along under your feet. Once when we turned on the air conditioner on the way to pick up my wedding dress, it spewed out orange dust from all the rust it had inside of it. I joked at the time "At least you know I'm not marrying you for the money." It shows I honestly thought of him as my best friend back in the early few years of our relationship when he was kind and attentive and not sick and angry.

He had come in the door to our Brentwood apartment that evening and I was on the phone with a friend from North Carolina whom I hadn't spoken to since I had moved to Los Angeles two years earlier. He had looked a bit down but given his moodiness it was not that surprising to me. He didn't say a word, just lay down on the couch and I continued talking to my friend. If he had waved at me or indicated something was wrong and he wanted to talk I would have gotten off the phone but as it was I couldn't tell anything was wrong. This went on another fifteen or twenty minutes. When I finally got off the phone I went to greet him and he roared at me:

"Why didn't you get off the phone!?" he yelled. I was shocked by this sudden and angry outburst. I jumped a little and backed away.

I told him he never asked me to and he asked: "Didn't you see I was upset?"

"Not really," I said, still shocked at how loudly he had yelled at me. It was the second time in our two-year relationship he had yelled so vehemently at me, the first being the very moment we pulled up outside his Westwood apartment when I had moved across country to live with him and start a new life in 1991. I was only twenty-two years old at the time, and I'd been so excited to change my stagnant post-high school life in sleepy Western North Carolina and move to exciting Los Angeles, California.

But I was a small-town country girl moving to a very big city so I had been upset that he had almost lost me on the 405 Freeway as I followed his car with mine on the busy nighttime freeways (this was before cell phones and GPS). I didn't know my way around L.A. so I was dependent on him to drive slowly, but he just zoomed along the freeway without even thinking of me, and I was struggling to keep up with him. It was late at night, and I was scared. I couldn't see the map, and I was unfamiliar with driving in L.A. traffic, having been there for exactly one hour at most.

I got out of the car once we pulled up to the darkened street in front of his apartment on Ashton Avenue just south of Wilshire Boulevard and said "Why did you drive like that? You almost lost me." I said it in a calm but baffled tone, but he just whirled around and loomed over me and screamed so viciously at me it startled me.

He frightened me. Before we had even set foot into our apartment and new life together, he had yelled at me to the point that I was afraid of him. I should have just gotten back in my car and gone back to North Carolina at that moment but I didn't. It was very late and I was exhausted. I told myself he was exhausted as well from a four-day road trip across country. I had put too much hope on this relationship to give up so quickly. I'd also been raised amidst bickering parents so this was "normal" for me. My logical mind overrode my internal panic button.

He had also acted a bit strangely a few days earlier in Oklahoma, our first stop when we had departed from North Carolina together. It was late and we were tired. We had everything I owned jammed into the hatch of my Ford Mustang LX. I had quit my bookkeeping and managerial job in a grocery store and left my beloved family behind. I had no money other than about $200 to buy gas along the way because all my earnings had gone to paying my way through night college, paying for my own braces and paying for my own car. He claimed he had no money either so we stayed in cheap motels that had questionable amenities.

This one had a pink interior, and around 2AM I heard a funny noise. I woke up to find a bug crawling across the floor of the motel so I screamed a little girl scream and stood up on the bed. It was then I noticed that my boyfriend was missing. That was unsettling, given that we had just embarked on our new life together a few hours earlier and I had only known him two years, and most of it had been as a long-distance romance with a few short vacations in those years getting to know each other and the rest by phone.

Had he abandoned me in the middle of the night in Oklahoma? Scared, I got out of bed and walked around the motel room looking for him, carefully avoiding the vermin crawling on the floor of this filth hole he had chosen for us to stay in. He wasn't in the bathroom, which was also pink tile, and he wasn't in the car parked outside the door. I was just about to call the front desk when way in the distant part of the parking lot I saw a figure sitting on the retaining wall near the street light.

It was my boyfriend, leaning his back up against a pole. I could see his silhouette, and it looked as if he was staring out into space. So I sleepily trudged across the parking lot in the wee hours of the morning to find out what he was doing.

"Oh, I was just thinking how my mom was born here and wondering what it felt like to be born here," he said. His mom had grown up in Texas so the time she spent in Oklahoma was minimal at best.

"But didn't you think if I woke up I'd be scared if you weren't there in a motel in the middle of Oklahoma on our first night of a new life together, moving across country?" I asked, still not understanding his lack of concern.

He laughed and said "No, I didn't think of that. I also didn't think you'd wake up."

All these years later I remember that he had a habit of doing this waking up in the middle of the night to think or prowl around. On my first visit to him in Los Angeles in December, 1989, he had asked me to sit on the edge of his floor-futon while he just stared at me for an uncomfortable amount of time. I'd asked him what he was doing, embarrassed and shy at this point (I was barely twenty years old), and he had said he was trying to remember my beauty. Then we had gone to sleep and when I woke up he was gone. I found him sitting in the living room watching TV in the middle of the night. I'd just flown across country to spend the holidays with him and he just kept spending the odd hours at night awake. I had never met anyone like this before. I was too young and uneducated at the time to realize he had a major sleep disorder that was indicative of an underlying illness. It made living with him very disruptive and lonely. (It's also why I'm doing very well living alone and raising my children all alone – because I'm now used to it.)

The next day in Oklahoma back in 1991, we had resumed our cross-country trek, and I saw places I'd never seen before, and I felt thrilled with new discoveries and the excitement of moving to Los Angeles where Bob Eubanks and Bob Barker echoed out every week "Live...from Burbank, California!" It all just seemed so exciting! I had always sat in my living room as a kid at the foot of the Blue Ridge Mountains wondering about this "Burbank" where all the fun things happen, and here I was moving nearby!

I looked over in my Mustang at my boyfriend, someone no one would ever think to pair me with because we were so different, and I felt lucky. Long-term relationships had eluded me for the most part because I was hard to please. The longest previous relationship I'd had was a year and there were always breakups in the midst of them. Such is young love, tempestuous and never pleased.

Yet here was this Ivy Leaguer with me, a blue-collar country girl from North Carolina who didn't even have her degree yet. I came from teenaged parents and even though I was an honor student at my high school, I had no support to go to college so I had been going part-time after working sixty-hour weeks. I was nowhere near achieving my degree as a result. Even his family asked him why he was moving in with a girl who was, to use their words, "just a cashier." (They didn't accept that I wasn't "just a cashier." They conveniently left off the part where I was a bookkeeper in a grocery store managing twenty employees, managing a hundred thousand dollar weekly budget at age nineteen all while going to college at night, paying my own way as I went.)

I bought my own car and paid for my own braces too. At one point I even drove myself to my wisdom teeth extraction surgery and waited a few hours in the dentist's chair for someone in my family to come get me and no one could because we were all poor, blue-collar workers with no free time away from work in the middle of a workday. That incident helped nudge me away from North Carolina and towards a better life in California. It wasn't the only factor but it helped lead me to my boyfriend's way of life out in California. I was forged from tough material and a hardscrabble upbringing but none of that mattered to my Ivy League boyfriend's family. In fact, it was a knock against me. In truth, I wanted to have a better life and I felt like he was the way to achieve that. He was kind, he was on his way to success and he was very devoted to me. I felt lucky. No one, including me at that young age, ever thought that maybe he was the lucky one.

He, while being very educated, didn't pay for much of anything on his own. But his family before even meeting me had deemed me unworthy. That changed after they met me, and his sister even said "If you don't marry Jerri, I will!" Years later he would feel particularly stung when I was the first one to publish a book and he has yet to publish one as far as I know. He didn't even come to my book signing for the anthology I was included in for mothers. He was also frustrated when I became very successful in politics, rising to the Congressional staffer level. Instead of being happy for me, he constantly tried to harm my career by calling me at work and once even showing up looking like a disheveled and unstable mess. He regularly accused me of having affairs with the men I spoke to and at the time I didn't realize it was projection since he was sleeping with the students he brought to dinner at my home under the guise of "sitters."

But as I was driving with him across country before any of this nastiness happened, I looked over at him again expecting to still feel all lucky and instead I became concerned because of what he was doing: in his hands he was holding a copy of the book "American Psycho."

"Why are you reading that?" I asked, a bit nervously as we sped along the near-deserted American desert. "It's a great book!" he had said. I didn't know anything about the book, just its disturbing title and book cover, and it hadn't yet become a disturbing movie starring Christian Bale that to this day has haunting imagery in my mind when I think of it, but for a new relationship that has been mainly a long distance one, it was unsettling. When he told me what it was about I secretly became on edge and slept with my mind half-awake until we reached Los Angeles. Then I told myself I was being silly and once again let logic override my concern.

There was so much that was incongruous with him though. He could read disturbing things and yet be nonchalant about it but if I dared question his driving style he became unraveled. His ego was so fragile.

So when he yelled at me on the couch a few years later when his car broke down I had just chocked it up to him being moody and exhausted, his ego so fragile, telling myself it was part of normal relationship arguments because I had grown up with parents who argued like The Costanzas on the TV show "Seinfeld."

Twice in my parents' marriage I had witnessed physical violence. They had stayed together so that taught me a level of behavior to tolerate, to stay together "for the kids." An entire culture has grown up around the sentiment that staying together is for the best in most cases. I no longer subscribe to that belief.

He continued to be upset about his car breaking down on Sunset Boulevard near our apartment but I, being the oldest child who is used to fixing things and keeping the peace in my intermittently argumentative childhood household, did what I always did – I tried to fix it.

"Honey, it's okay. That car was on its last legs and we work together so now we'll just share a ride and when your schedule is different, I'll just drop you off at UCLA to teach and I'll pick you up on my way back from the lab" I said. Few things in life hold me down. I roll with life's stressors and make the best of it.

He was having none of it. I now realize he just wanted me to listen to him bitch all night but after doing that for a few minutes I felt it was time to problem-solve. I'm not a wallower. I'm practical and I just do what needs to be done. I may complain a bit but then I roll up my sleeves and get it done. Besides, we didn't have the money to fix the car and we didn't need a second one anyway. I had a relatively new Mustang LX with a nice sunroof that had much better gas mileage – and we worked together! His job as a teaching assistant did not afford us the luxury of two cars anyway. It sucked but it would be okay.

But I failed to realize this early in our relationship how hard it is for him to let go of anything…

This convincing him that everything would be fine went on for another few minutes until I was desperate to cheer him up. He was spiraling downward and refusing to listen to me so I got close to his face so he would actually stop whining and catastrophizing and look at me as he was lying on the couch but the moment I got close to him he took his left hand and lightly backhanded me across the face, kind of like a swat like one would swat at a pesky house fly. Unfortunately, his wedding ring hit me right in the mouth. I'm not sure he meant to hit me in the face because he was looking through me rather than at me but he did mean to swat me away when I approached him, of that much I'm certain.

Stunned, I jumped back, grabbed my mouth and ran to the bedroom. *I could taste the blood in my mouth.*

He got up from the couch in horror saying "Oh my God! I'm so sorry! I didn't mean to do that!" Two decades later a mutual friend would confess to me that when they were in college together (which is how I met my husband when I was a colleague of the friend) a similar thing happened to him when my husband had a girl break up with him. My friend had tried to console him and get him out of his funk, so to speak, and when my friend got close to him, he attacked him by punching him repeatedly.

Finally, my friend got him to stop attacking him and it was as if my husband (whom I didn't know at the time and had yet to meet him) was coming out of a trance. He apologized profusely and they surprisingly remained friends. This shows how convincing my husband could be and also how kind people tend to downplay disturbing occurrences in the hopes of keeping the peace and not cutting out people from our lives unnecessarily. We all do it, both males and females. This example proves it.

Sadly, my friend never told me this story until recently. So many people have protected my husband over the years, all out a sense of decency, loyalty and privacy, which to a certain degree is respectable. I get that but I'm starting to believe **we need a cultural conversation about when it is time to divulge what we previously thought of as a sacred boundary:**

When do the rights of others get impeded with knowledge withholding? When is it our duty to protect the endangered? When is privacy protection a moral quagmire?

It's a philosophical quandary but one that possesses the potential to actually save lives. Maybe a bit of personal privacy loss is worth it if people get the help they need and others are fully informed of risks. It's a slippery slope, I'm well aware, but I think it's a national conversation about mental health that we can no longer ignore.

Meanwhile, back in Brentwood with the broken car and the face smack in 1992 or 1993, I began freaking out and I jumped onto the bed after running down the short hallway from the living room. He was right behind me and landed on me, causing my face to get a rug burn on the comforter as we slid across the fabric. I am 5'4" and was maybe 115 pounds at the time, half his size. His body was wrapped around mine in a tackle, completely covering mine, but I am surprisingly strong and fast, especially when scared.

Still panicked, I scooted out from under his grasp and crawled backward away from him, facing him the entire time, afraid to turn my back on him, shaking and crying hysterically.

I was just waiting for him to come after me and I had my fists clenched ready for it but he stood up and backed away and acted like I was the crazy one. He muttered something like "Oh my God, you are really freaking out." I didn't realize then it was a form of gaslighting he was subjecting me to, a tactic narcissists will use to make their targets appear crazy when they themselves are the diabolical ones. I hadn't obtained my degree in Psychology yet so I didn't recognize any of this, not his bipolar disorder, nor his narcissism and manipulation. It also points to his reluctance to accept responsibility for behaviors that are less than flattering, which suggests a very fragile ego.

I sat there a long time on the bed trying to decide what to do. I remember looking out the window at the red brick condominium beside of our building, wondering if I could climb out the window and run over there. I didn't know anyone in there so I just sat on the bed until I had stopped crying. He had isolated me far away from my family an entire continent away. I was all alone in this...

Somehow the situation diffused itself, and we went to bed. He had told me he was just trying to catch me to explain he didn't mean to smack me and in truth, he did not have an angry look on his face as he landed on me on the bed. He had looked scared himself so I believed him. I honestly think to this day that he did not mean to hit me that day, that he just wanted me out of his space, which I was in truth invading while trying to calm him down. So I think of it as an accident but one that when viewed in the context of what happened twenty years later is troubling and certainly foreshadowing of future violence. This is just me trying hard to be objective and to truly analyze what happened that day. If he had violent intent in his face then I would have left him immediately. I'll never know the real truth because I don't have his mind or his heart (thank goodness for that).

I think there was a lot of apologizing and him convincing me that I had overreacted and that I was at fault for not getting off the phone when he was in not so obvious distress. I was young so I fell for it. I'm also very kind and I hate conflict. I guess I grew up with so much of it I like to brush it under the rug. I also realize now many decades later that people are complex – they are not all good and not all bad – and that is what makes them so maddening and prone to get away with things for a long time before things fall apart.

Even murderers on death row are capable of sparing a bird.

The next morning was our flight to North Carolina for the holidays. I got up and looked at myself in the mirror and was very saddened by what I saw.

The left side of both my upper and lower lips was swollen and I had a burn mark all up the left side of my face and my left eye was slightly swollen. I remember looking at the girl in the mirror and feeling sorry for her. I thought "So now you're one of *those* girls…"

It didn't seem real. It seemed like the movies, a very bad movie that I didn't want to be starring in. It was not the life I had envisioned for myself when I left my family behind in North Carolina, when I had slowly backed out of my beloved Maw Maw Johnson's driveway in East Bend, North Carolina with her leaning out the door of the back porch sadly watching me pull away from her. I loved her so much so it shows how much hope I had for things with my boyfriend in California…

I had married an Ivy League-educated doctor, and we summered on Cape Cod and Martha's Vineyard. *There was no hitting in this dream life.*

And yet here I was, standing in front of the mirror looking at my injured face. It would be a foreshadowing of what was to happen again but only much more severely twenty years later.

"But he didn't mean to" I whispered to myself and stayed in the relationship. We had fun on the trip to see my family and the incident faded along with the burns and scrapes on my face.

I was just twenty-four years old this first time, my life just getting started…we didn't have kids yet. "I could just leave him," I thought a few times but quickly dismissed it. I kept rationalizing to myself "He said he didn't mean to and he wasn't looking at me as he swiped his hand to push me away. It wasn't like he looked me in the eye and backhanded me. It was an instinct to swat someone away if they get too close to your face," I said to myself. He was my best friend, after all…

So I shook it off. I rationalized it until it went away in my mind. I put on some makeup and concealer and caught my flight. The moment my mother saw my face she looked concerned and asked: "What happened?"

"Oh, I just got a rug burn messing around" I said. To my surprise, my mother didn't inquire further. Either I'm a very good actress or the years of marital discord she endured caused her not to recognize the trouble I was in. It's also possible she didn't want to get involved in my marriage or she doubted her own suspicions. (It has taught me though that if my daughter ever has a mark on her body I will push and pry until I get at the deep truth, even at the risk of offending her. I will lean in with each of my children's relationships because no one at all leaned into mine. Experience is the best teacher.)

And nothing else happened again for two years. My husband got a job as an EEG analyst and he finished his Ph.D. at UCLA, even getting nominated for best dissertation. He was always a very intelligent person. And when I left him in 1995, it was a friendly split that lasted three months until we got back together. And that's when his plan of slow revenge began taking shape…

CHAPTER 4:
"MENACING IS HARD TO PROVE."

Bam! Bam! Bam!

He was knocking loudly on the door of the guest room on July 5th, 2012.

"What is it? I have to go to work tomorrow!" I pleaded with him. "It's 2 o'clock in the morning. I have to get some sleep!"

"Let me in this room right now!" he demanded. "My friends have all told me you're a man and I want you to prove to me you're a woman! Come out here and show me your pussy!"

"Look, you're scaring me" I admitted. "I think we just need to get you some counseling and we'll talk about this in the morning, okay?" I said, trying to sound calm but inside I was still freaking out.

"Just let me in the room and show me your pussy and prove to me you're a woman because I don't think you're my wife!" he screamed.

At this point, I began trying to lift the windows again, and he heard me so I crept back to the bed trying to find anything under it to help me.

"Do you want a divorce?" he asked accusingly.

Exasperated, and just so done and yet still somehow thinking I was dealing with what was ostensibly a grownup who could see the writing on the wall, I finally admitted the truth.

"Yes," I said sadly. "I just can't do this anymore."

And at that very moment he groaned and made this sound that football players make as they go in for a tackle and broke the door down in one quick movement.

As soon as he got in the room, I stood up to defend myself. I thought maybe I could run past him, but he was blocking my path. The moment he got close to me he punched me right in the face. It all happened so quickly.

I didn't know it at the time, but he had just broken my nose. I had never been punched in the face before, and I was completely stunned. I never realized you actually do see stars go "Pow!" like in the comics and in cartoons.

Then before I could react he grabbed me by the hair and shoved my head hard down onto the wooden chair beside the bed, a chair that was ironically a wedding gift from a colleague in our UCLA lab where we used to work together as a married couple. Little did I know then that one day that chair would be drenched in my blood. Then he did it again.

He had turned the light on when he entered the room, and the force of it was so strong he had knocked the facing off the door and the mirror bracket off the wall.

But he wasn't done with me yet. He was just getting started in treating me like a punching bag, intent on ending me.

He picked me up and threw me on the bed and tried to rip my pajama pants off of me.

"Show me your pussy!" he demanded. I had never seen anyone so angry in my life. He looked like a crazed lunatic. I guess in truth, he was.

I began kicking him as hard as I could, trying to shove my feet up under his chest but he was so fast and so angry, so strong and with this white foam spewing out of his mouth behind his tightly gritted teeth.

As this was happening, a part of me was thinking how unreal this all was. I was in shock and disbelief even as I was fully engaged in fighting him off of me.

He slammed me up against the wall hard and then backed away and stood at the edge of the bed staring at me, waiting for me to make the next move. The room was painted this ugly, shiny Granny Smith Apple Green (his choice, not mine, another argument over that years earlier) and it made him look even sicker in the fluorescent light.

Then he lunged on top of me, and I could see more white foam coming out of his mouth. His face was so close to mine I thought the foam was going to fall onto my face, so I turned my head to the side. He was disgusting and terrifying, like that scene in the movie "Alien" when Sigourney Weaver is captured by the alien. I had no idea at the time that he was high on bath salts and the foam was coming from him due to those mind-altering drugs which have caused some people to bite the ears and face off of people.

He began pawing at my pajamas again, trying to rape me. He was going to get the sex from me that I had denied him earlier that night and that was that.

I began pleading with him "Look, look! Let me show you my phone, and I'll prove to you I'm me. Let me call someone, and they'll tell you! Please, please don't hurt me," I cried. (It makes me sick to this day just recalling ever begging that "man" for anything, for ever feeling that vulnerable and desperate. Every now and then I'll be trying to take a nap and a flashback of that moment will enter my mind. It happens much less now, maybe twice a year, but for a very long time it was every day and every night. I slept with weapons just to feel safe. PTSD is real, and I'm so grateful for the wonderful counseling I received from Janet Chaize of the Willow Domestic Violence Center and from Kathy Elliott in private practice.)

He didn't even speak to me he just growled more and looked at me with such craziness in his eyes, like a wild animal. He began choking me at one point, and I lost consciousness briefly. When he let go of me, I instinctively fought back, frantically and just as wildly as he did, just as quickly as he did. He wasn't expecting that, but I was pure adrenaline at that moment, my survival mode kicking in strongly.

Somehow, I scrambled out from under him and stood up and began to reach to my lower left to grab my tote bag, which I had taken with me the night before to the Conesus Lake annual "Ring Of Fire" celebration on July 3rd, 2012. I took the children each year to see the fireworks and red flares the lakeside homeowners light to celebrate Independence Day on New York's Finger Lakes. He would never go with us so we would go with another family. It was just another in a long line of examples of the two of us living increasingly separate lives.

In the tote bag I had packed a lot of things, including food, a book, my keys, my wallet and flashlights for all of us and full water bottles for each of us as well. It was a very heavy bag, and I hadn't had a chance to unpack it because we'd gotten home after midnight and the next day I was so busy preparing for the family cookout for the Fourth of July holiday.

I had awakened early on July 4th and headed to Walmart after lunch to buy cookout supplies because he had refused to help me out. He wasn't bothering me, but I was so miserable with him by this point. He had been yelling at us for a year, and in the past two weeks, he had been threatening me, although I couldn't prove it.

Two weeks before July 4th, 2012, he and I had an argument over something on the weekend, and he had picked me up and thrown me out the front door on a Sunday morning. Neighbors across the street on Buffalo Road had seen it, but I didn't know them well, and they had stood up as soon as he'd thrown me outside, and then they had gone inside and shut the door.

I remember thinking "Really? Nothing? No help?" And so I had stood outside yelling at him to let me back in because I knew he was in there alone with my children. I started to walk to a neighbor's house to call for help, and he saw me.

He had stuck his head out the window when I did and screamed: "The first cop dies!"

I didn't have my phone so I couldn't call anyone and at this point what could I say? "Oh, hey officer, my husband just picked me up and locked me outside the house." There wasn't much actionable offense there. I had already spoken to an officer I'd run into in a coffee shop and asked him about yelling, and he had said: "Menacing is hard to prove." I'd called my divorce lawyer, and he'd said the same thing and many legal professionals have since confirmed this. (This is a reason the Violence Against Women Act's provision that verbal abuse is domestic violence is so critical because it's not merely name calling, it is verbal threats to harm you or kill you and your children. Many argue that we can't arrest people for name calling, but verbal abuse is actual threats to harm or kill and it wears away at the feeling of safety of a person over time, leading them to not report abuse and causing the abuse to escalate to physical eventually in many cases. Verbal abuse is a terror in the home, and that is abuse.)

"You have to get evidence" they had all said but how could I get evidence of someone throwing me out the door and threatening me? It happened so quickly there was no way to record it unless someone passing by just happened to be recording. I did keep a journal, but I'm not sure how much they're worth in court. It's still my recollection against his.

So I didn't think there was much I could do. I was just trying frantically to save up enough money to get my children and me to a safe place. (In retrospect, there was no such place if I had left him and if he was still living in the area because he would have never accepted us leaving him.) We didn't have any family in the state, and I didn't have close enough friends to ask them to risk their own safety to allow us to stay with them. I also didn't feel comfortable asking them. I was embarrassed, it was disruptive to the kids' lives, and I thought I could handle it all by myself, a habit of being the oldest child. I didn't have anywhere else to go. Plus, he hadn't hit me, he had just thrown me out of the house so what evidence did I have? After all, menacing is hard to prove…

The next weekend we'd gotten into another argument, and he'd thrown me out of the side door by the mudroom. No one saw it this time because the neighbors on the side street across the road had moved a year or so earlier and the house was vacant but as soon as he let me back in I marched right up to him and kicked him in the balls three times lightning fast, one right after the other. He had laughed at me and said "Man, you're fast and freakishly strong" and I said "Yes I am and you better not forget it! You ever touch me again you'll find out just how strong I am!" He just looked at me with amusement and chuckled, but I was fuming with defiance.

I reported these behaviors to my new boss at work over tears because I just couldn't concentrate at work one day and to my relief, he began helping me plan my escape. We both knew I was in potential danger so he had me to call Safe Journey, a shelter his church worked with which has now merged with Stand Up Guys to form Resolve, a group now focused on domestic violence prevention. They advised me to hide a set of keys and important papers, pack "go bags" in the trunk of my car for each of us, and to find emergency shelter. When I could not find any shelter nearby, I chose two friends in my mind that my spouse didn't know about for potential future safe houses. I went to them each and told them what was going on, and they agreed to hide us should it ever become necessary. A part of me thought that I was overreacting, that he, a Methodist minister's son and a guidance counselor and artist's son, would never do anything so violent. But I wasn't overreacting – I was underreacting. In retrospect, I get mad at myself sometimes, but hindsight really is twenty/twenty. When you're in the middle of it, you can't see the full breadth of the storm…

Back on the hard tile guest room floor around 2:30 AM on July 5th, 2012, his hands now pressed tightly around my neck, I saw the light fading all around me and images of my four children looking down at me. Suddenly, I was in a casket with the sun filtering from behind my children's heads as I was being lowered into the ground. They were getting farther and farther away from me, and I could not reach them. It was the saddest I've ever felt in my life, like this all-encompassing sad, heavy hug wrapping around me, silencing everything and making me immobile. The world got very quiet, and my heart got very still. Fear faded into resignation. Then the darkness came.

CHAPTER 5:
2:45 IN THE MAD, MAD MORNING

Earlier that evening we had argued as we had most evenings in the past year. He was an irritable man and nothing could stop his rage once he got going. The most insignificant thing could set him off – a child's request or something someone said in an online forum. But most of all, anything I said or did, or didn't do, released this fury inside of him. He would roar so loudly and so long that the neighbors next door would get up from their patio seats and go inside, leaving me all alone to deal with him, embarrassed, stressed and afraid. And that's what he wanted – he wanted everyone to be afraid of him and they were, even neighbors he barely knew would cross the road to avoid him on the sidewalks, something I didn't know at the time but was told years later.

It hadn't always been that way though. When I married him, he was a very nice preacher's boy - tall, dark and some would say handsome. I just found him funny and smart and very attentive to me, something that at the time I must have needed, having just come away from a bad breakup with the first significant adult relationship I'd ever had. He seemed worldly, had gone to an Ivy League college and was just returning from a summer in Hawaii working with dolphins for an EEG lab. It all sounded so futuristic to me and he sold that image hard.

He was spontaneous and silly. We laughed so much and he accepted me quickly just the way I was. I'd met him through my former boyfriend because they went to college together. So when we broke up, I wanted to get away for a while. I called my future husband and asked if I could come visit him in Los Angeles for a weekend. He readily agreed and I flew across the country expecting some escape.

I didn't expect him to make a pass at me but that's just what he did. I was so depressed over my breakup that I just went with it. It wasn't so bad either. It was just mindless escape. We watched movies and toured UCLA campus and talked for hours. When we'd first met he accepted me without judgment, taking the frozen ice pops I offered him in the hot Southern heat that my more mature boyfriend made fun of me for having. I also was prone to just launching into handstands back then and my future spouse was enamored with my energy and girl-like youthfulness, even though I was nineteen years old when we met.

I do recall one moment in that first meeting though that gave me pause: he had stated that he couldn't sleep so he stayed up late with my then boyfriend's roommate to smoke. I hate smoking and I later learned it wasn't cigarettes they were puffing. I put a stop to that once we began dating because I didn't like the way he acted on it. In retrospect, it should have been a deal breaker but I was so impressed by his credentials that I let my standards slip, a huge mistake in my life. I was young and more tolerant of wild things back then I guess.

A few months later in 1990 I traveled to see him out in Los Angeles again and before I knew it, I had a new boyfriend who lived on the opposite coast. When I moved in with him two years later, we traveled a lot and played sports every day. I learned a lot of new things from him and I adapted a lot of his quirky practices until I grew tired of them and asked him to start being a bit more responsible.

I got him to cut his hair and to start dressing like a grownup. I got him to adopt regular work hours and start eating regular food at regular intervals. I was trying to turn him into a grownup. I wanted to eventually have children so I wanted a man who could hold down a job and a regular schedule. I wince now remembering what I was trying to do.

You can't change people. You shouldn't even try. Change has to come from within. But I was young and stupid and since I was the oldest child and he was the youngest, our dynamic worked except for this small little fact: the man was hiding madness inside of him that everyone in his family and close friends knew about and never told me, even after we told them of our plans to have children together.

I should have known to end the relationship early on though because on our first trip together, when I was moving across the country from

North Carolina to California to be with him, the moment we got to his apartment was when he yelled at me on the street so loudly that I jumped back in fear. I would learn over the years that in his mind it is a cardinal sin in his narcissistic world to question him or chastise or criticize him in any way. There is no constructive criticism in his mind, there is only denial of his flaws. He could be the kindest person you've ever met but if you dared insult him or if he even perceived that you were insulting him he could turn into an angry, vindictive and relentless monster. He held vendettas against colleagues that lasted for years. His revenge against them was so convoluted and twisted and petty I was ashamed to be with him after I learned his ways. I began pulling away from him emotionally at that time.

But before we had kids he had only revealed his meteoric temper a few times and these episodes were so far in between each other that I had downplayed the dangerousness of them. It was like having a scab that occasionally gets picked open and bleeds and then over time it heals over only to be picked at again later on.

It was very Ernest Hemingway-esque, like in his novella "The Sun Also Rises" with its "gradually, then suddenly" outcome. A character in the book asks "How did you go broke?" and the response was "gradually, then suddenly." People ask me "How did he go mad?" and my reply is "gradually, then suddenly." It's the same with our marriage: how did it fall apart? Gradually, then suddenly. Gradually, then suddenly works for a lot of life's moments, whether good ones or bad ones. It is especially true in domestic violence.

I had also grown up with parents who argued a lot and so I thought this was normal behavior. As a child I would run outside and play or go to a friend's house when my folks started arguing but out in Los Angeles I didn't have very many places I could escape to and feel safe. Every time I mentioned moving across country to be closer to family he refused to even consider it. He gave reasons that sounded legitimate (no jobs, he hated the South and its conservative politics since he's from liberal Massachusetts, the heat and the bugs) but in truth he was excellent at isolating me. He didn't want me anywhere near people who loved me and who could help me leave him.

As the months wore on in 2011, a year after my boss, a Congressman, had resigned in a nationally televised scandal and all staffers lost their jobs as a result, the strain of losing my high-paying job's salary began to take its toll on our marriage. While I searched for a new job with the stigma of Congressional scandal following me everywhere I applied, he was sinking deeper and deeper into debt and depression, both of which he hid from me.

He would not show a crack in his façade until August 2011 on the Massachusetts Turnpike. We had been in Sandwich, Massachusetts touring the glass museum on our way to the beach and my middle son had asked for a tiny glass octopus. This is a child who never asks for anything, who is so sweet and shy and respectful at all times, so I wanted to get it for him. My spouse refused so I began to go in and buy it myself. It was just a $9 trinket. But my husband intervened and said he would go get it.

Once he got back to the car he was furious and slung the bag at my little son, who was only nine or ten years old at the time, an age when toys are still magical. He's a very sweet child and sensitive too so when his father became angry the one time he'd ever really asked for anything, it hurt him and he began to cry. I was furious with my husband for his behavior.

As we pulled onto the Turnpike in rush hour traffic I asked him why he'd been so angry over a tiny thing. An argument ensued (he claimed "they" wouldn't wait on him although I'd seen the line and it wasn't very long at all) and suddenly he began swerving wildly across traffic lanes and screamed at me "Do you want me to kill us all!?" Then the children all began screaming and crying and we were trapped in this car with him driving erratically. I had to do everything I could think of to calm him down but I knew then that we were in deep trouble.

I had to spend an entire week with him in Maine after this incident, where he acted like everything was fine, playing football on the beach with him going over the top in his attempts to be all cheerful after a day earlier threatening to kill us all. We slept in separate beds at the cottage and soon after we would begin sleeping in separate beds in our home. This moment on the Massachusetts Turnpike began a year-long downward spiral both in his mind and in our marriage. I was done and my escape plan was now developing. But first I needed a job.

CHAPTER 6:
EVERY STREET USA

Still lying on the cold, forest green tile floor of the guest room, I was reawakened when he let go of my throat to grab my phone, which had been in my left hand. At that moment my heart pounded OUT of my chest and I somehow got my feet onto his chest and used all the strength in my runner's legs to shove him off of me. He went soaring into the wall and I scrambled to my feet and tried to run out of the bedroom. Disoriented and not realizing I was suffering from a broken nose and many other painful injuries due to the adrenaline coursing through my body, I hit the wall of the bedroom just left of the door very hard.

Somehow I shakily dragged myself out into the hallway hitting that wall as well. It was as if I was in a tilted room because I couldn't run in a straight line. I kept veering left. (I didn't know then that I had been hit on top of the head so hard with that flashlight-filled tote bag that my C4 and C5 vertebrae had been compressed. I would end up in months of traction and physical therapy to relieve the pressure on my vertebrae, which caused my right hand to go numb at work while typing or when driving for nearly six months post-attack. He had also attacked me so viciously that my right arm had nerve damage at the junction with my shoulder. I've lost some strength in that arm and no longer do archery but I hope to return to it someday. He had also grabbed my legs and arms so tightly that I would have deep vein bruises for months after the attack and would have to give up my beloved running for a long time. My physical therapist couldn't treat my arms and legs due to the risk of dislodging blood clots. None of these physical injuries could compare to the damage he did to me emotionally and psychologically though. Those wounds took years to overcome.)

I ran down to the mudroom through a long maroon-colored hallway which seemed even longer given the circumstances. It seemed like that hallway in the Jack Nicholson movie "The Shining," and I was in the "redrum."

Unfortunately, there were three locks to open once I got to the mudroom so I was still trapped running away from a madman, just like a scene in another horror movie only my nightmare was very real and it wasn't on Elm Street - it was on Every Street USA.

CHAPTER 7:
"TOO MANY MADMEN"

What happened to me on July 5th, 2012 is a scene played out all over the streets of America every day. In the time it has taken to read this sentence, three American women will have been slammed from the land of the living through the door of the dead. I was almost one of them. But my story of surviving madmen didn't start there - it began four years earlier in a political roundtable in Rochester, New York at the Democrat and Chronicle newspaper with then New York Governor Eliot Spitzer.

I had always loved politics and ran for every office in grade school and won all but one of my races so it was no surprise I pursued it once my kids were all school-age. I no longer wanted to be elected but instead wanted to cover the officials in the press. I snagged a job at the local paper as a community member on their Editorial Board and was thrilled to learn the governor of New York was coming to visit so we could interview him. I practically had to pinch myself I was so excited. I had always wanted to be deeply involved in shaping my community and tapped into the pulse of the society I lived in. I had always wanted to make a difference.

Governor Spitzer entered the room with a confident stride, much shorter than I had anticipated with a slight frame, far smaller in stature than he appeared on TV. He was wearing a sharp dark suit and, to our surprise, trailing behind him was a coterie of very young women. It wasn't clear what they were there for other than looking tan and polished. Each of them carried a slim notepad but I didn't see them writing anything down. It was as if they were props, both the women and the notepads. First impressions are very powerful and revealing and this case was no exception, as we as a nation would find out soon.

Given that I was of the same political persuasion as Governor Spitzer I soon became his favorite reporter in the room and after the meeting he approached me and invaded my body space so quickly that I startled and jumped back a little. I was young then, slim, blonde and a toned runner. I was also a friendly voice for his interview because I agreed with his stance on the issues while still trying to be objective. My editor saw this so she came over to join us for a chat and acted like an unspoken safety buffer between us. I remember being surprised at how aggressively he engaged me, and in such close proximity, but I wanted to cover the work he was doing so I continued engaging with his office.

A few months later, after many positive pieces were written by me, Governor Spitzer agreed to my request to hold a weekly Sunday morning radio show with a colleague and me. It was the big break I'd been waiting for! Finally I could leave my husband and support my children by myself.

Two days later Governor Spitzer resigned.

I didn't know what was going on but his staffer, Jack Downey, whom I'd been working with on scheduling and logistics of the radio show agreement, suddenly stopped replying to me a few days earlier. Apparently, according to the news, Governor Spitzer had inappropriate relationships with women outside the bounds of his marriage and outside the boundaries of the law.

I was devastated. First, I had lost what we all thought was a good governor and secondly, I had lost a big career opportunity. But I had narrowly dodged a bullet because of unsavory actions by the governor with various females, which he admitted to in a televised news conference with his very beautiful and accomplished wife standing by his side. She had expected greatness from him when she married him I'm sure (don't we all expect that of our spouses?) but what she got was sadly something similar to what I got when I married my own Ivy Leaguer: a madman.

I shuddered to think how my career could have gone had the radio show actually happened. Who knows what would have transpired, based on the sordid details leaked to the press about his resignation? I had already seen evidence of his aggressive style when my fellow Editorial Board member and dear friend, Alex Zapesochny, a Libertarian, challenged Governor Spitzer to a legal debate in one of our meetings. "You wanna play lawyer?" Spitzer had challenged him. "We can play lawyer." He had a gleam in his eye and he clearly loved the aggressive back and forth. And then it was on.

The room watched them go at each other back and forth as if a Wimbledon match was playing out and it was the first time I'd seen Spitzer's verve in action. He didn't like having his prowess questioned but he also loved the challenge of proving his intellect and command of the understanding of law. He enjoyed the thrill of contention. This guy was a thrill seeker and he needed to win, he had to win.

I was devastated that my big break in my career had dissolved but I was also relieved to have avoided a scandal and possibly more trouble. I thought "I should try Congress. It will be better, more professional..."

So that autumn I met with the local Monroe County Democratic Committee Chair, New York Assemblyman Joe Morelle, and he sent me to volunteer for the campaign for Jon Powers, a young Army veteran in Buffalo, New York. We fought a very hard race but ultimately lost to the wealthy Republican candidate, Chris Lee, who would resign from Congress shortly into his first term for unsavory actions with females outside of his marriage as well.

Strike two for New York elected madmen. Surely it wouldn't happen again. So I kept on seeking work in politics because I believed in its mission.

I joined the campaign for Navy Veteran Eric Massa who was running for a second time against incumbent Congressman Randy Kuhl for New York's 29th Congressional District, which stretched from the Southern Tier all the way up to Rochester over two hours' drive away. It was a huge district geographically but because of this it was very diverse in its registration with an R+4 advantage to the Republicans.

The race was a close one with seemingly hourly challenges to either being this close to being kicked out of contention or this close to really driving the win home. It was so exciting to be part of a team that bled blue. I was surrounded by like-minded age cohorts who had so much verve and passion for what we all believed in. I would go home each night exhausted but happy to be living out my dreams. I was working with some of the best in the business, from Communications with Justin Schall and Jared Smith, to Organizer Donna McLean and media wizard Paul Novak. It felt amazing. We worked relentlessly and so did Massa. His command of concepts was quick and impressive on the go. He could zing one-liners in and quickly understand how an issue impacted the whole of the district. He could thread the needle of that mixed district better than anyone I'd ever seen.

But part of how we won was due to Representative Kuhl stating in public months earlier that he had considered "packing" against his constituents who had protested at his local Congressional office. I had reported this story during my Editorial Board stint at the Democrat and Chronicle newspaper because he had said this during an Editorial Board meeting. I went home thinking he was a madman for saying such a thing and later learned he had actually once threatened his wife and friends at a dinner party with a gun, information that was readily available to the public in court filings.

When he said he was also considering packing against his constituents when they exercised their right to protest, the story I wrote went national. At the time I didn't know about his dinner party debacle. I was simply reporting what a sitting Congressman said to our Editorial Board, a topic that he brought up himself as the meeting was ending.

I'll never forget it. We had finished our question and answer session and he stood up and put his hands in his suit pockets kind of in a stretching manner and said "I'm surprised none of you asked me about the protesting constituents." At that moment I pounced.

"Well, since you brought it up..." I said, "what do you have to say about that?"

Then he reached back and made a motion as if he was a gunslinger and said, "I was thinking about packing against them."

I drove home and immediately posted my story and left for vacation in North Carolina with my family, not thinking another thing about it.

A day later my phone blew up. The story had gone national and the Democratic Congressional Campaign Committee was running wild with it. My editors were being bombarded by Representative Kuhl's office asking for me to be fired and for the story to be retracted.

My editor called me on vacation asking me to recant my story but I refused to back down from my story, I refused to back down from the truth. Pressure was put on me and quite heavily because editors, who are after all paid employees, have to be able to entice future elected officials into the office for interviews and if the paper gets a reputation as being "unfriendly" to the officials, then they are under no obligation to come in. It's a flaw in the newspaper for-profit business.

Thankfully, the newspaper's President, Michael Kaine, defended my story and the truth because he was in the room when Representative Kuhl said it. He didn't bow to pressure or sweep the truth under the rug. He championed truth and he has forever earned my respect because of it. He and I both knew this was no "Kuhl Hand Fluke." This was a pattern with this man, as demonstrated in publicly available court documents and in public editorial board meetings.

Frustratingly, another editor ran a counter story stating something like I was "just" a community member of the Editorial Board and not a professional writer. It stung because I had simply written the truth of what the Congressman himself had stated in public in an Editorial Board meeting filled with writers. I didn't lose my unpaid volunteer job but Kuhl lost his Congressional seat in the election due to his own actions and his own words.

When a public official, who is elected by the constituents, locks his public-funded office because he doesn't want to hear their protests and states in public that he is thinking of "packing" against them, it should be no surprise that he is not re-elected to represent the people (because he wasn't representing them). It aptly demonstrated the mindset of power and control and the voters removed that power and control from him. Power and control is a big thing with madmen.

(When we were being sworn into office a few months later down in Washington, D.C., having earned a surprising upset victory, someone brought bottles of champagne to a party later that night that were manufactured by a brand named "Kuhl." We all made sure to take a sip.)

To my delight I was suddenly a Press Secretary in the U.S. House of Representatives! Finally, something good had come from my work in politics. We were going to change the world. We were going to be bi-partisan and get things done. Boy, did I have a lot to learn about politics.

Within the first few weeks of working for the congressman I saw his rage, lies and bias. Gone were the smiles for the cameras and the love for little children at parades. No, behind closed doors what I witnessed was petty scorekeeping against perceived threats and rivals, Machiavellian machinations designed to "win" (what it was he was winning is beyond me), and tantrums that involved his jugular sticking out so far I was a little frightened of him. I've since learned this is a common tactic madmen use: fear and domination, power and control.

However, the first time he threatened my job I stood up to him. It's sad to think back now how often my job and those of my colleagues was threatened by him. It was how he tried to rule over us, through intimidation, through power and control. It was very militaristic, maybe because he was a Navy veteran, but I always had a tight feeling in my stomach after I got to know his style.

When I had been on the campaign trail with him I was mainly able to chat with him a minute here or there. He was always on the move, determined to win, and he was in fact a very hard worker. I've never seen such a whirlwind of activity and intellectual curiosity.

My first impression of Eric Massa had been at the Monroe County Designating Convention event where candidates were announced for campaigns. His name was announced and he burst out from the crowd and marched down the center aisle towards the stage with this proud and happy look on his face. He reminded me of the actor Danny DeVito. It was quite theatrical and I remember asking someone "Who is that?" I had no idea then that a few months later I'd be campaigning for him once Jon Powers lost his race for the 26th Congressional primary candidacy.

After the voters had cast their ballots there was a recount due to how close the election was. We had run in an "R+4" district, meaning that Republicans had a registration advantage over Democrats. Massa had run against Kuhl previously and narrowly lost so he used that loss to improve his game and it paid off. My story for the Editorial Board, written well before I ever knew about Eric Massa, certainly helped change the narrative and it so impressed Massa that when my writing stint was over (it was only a year-long appointment), he happily offered me a job.

He hosted a party at his beautiful home in Corning, New York so that all staffers could meet each other and so we could celebrate the results of the recount. It was in December 2008 and I was treated like royalty by Massa. He walked me around to all the staffers and he told funny stories. I felt like I was living a fairy tale. The kitchen was filled with wonderful food and everyone was in a cheerful mood, having just won an upset victory in the United States House of Representatives. When his chief of staff sat me down in the study of the stately home he told me the congressman wanted me to be his part-time personal assistant or secretary. I was not pleased.

"I'm his press secretary," I stated firmly. "And I want full-time." The information was taken to Massa and he didn't argue with me but instead agreed. A few weeks earlier I had shown up uninvited to a Veterans Day service at Brighton High School, just days after the contested election, and immediately stepped in beside of Massa and began performing the duties of a press secretary, placing him with reporters in front of the cameras and answering their questions off-camera. I carried his things for him as I directed reporters to our next event. It showed Massa what I could do and it also showed initiative.

It really hits home the point that a lot of life is about showing up. I was the only one vying for that position that showed up that day. I also stayed overnight in Corning after the election and woke up early to greet

Massa at the campaign headquarters to tell him in person I wanted to work for him. I showed him early on I was going to ask for what I wanted in life.

I joined the wonderful Communications Director, Jared Smith, on the staff and together the two of us created a formidable freshman press team in Congress, so well-run that Representative Steny Hoyer's and Speaker Nancy Pelosi's offices began using our press practices as examples for other freshman offices to follow.

But all was not a fairy tale…

I was driving Massa to the airport in Rochester in late January or early February 2009 and he was angry about something and refused to back down. It was Super Bowl Sunday and he had called me into work along with Jared Smith to hash out some messaging instead of letting us have a Sunday off to watch the national pastime party. Something had been said and he wanted to retaliate in the news on camera and in the paper (this was a constant thing with him to the point that my phone never stayed silent the entire eighteen months I worked for him, beginning as early as 5:30 a.m. and ringing late at night and on most holidays). I disagreed with his stance and told him so. Jared disagreed with him as well back in the office before I was driving him to the airport.

Massa got so angry as I was driving him I thought he was going to strike me on the 390 interstate but I kept my eyes on the road and my hands on the wheel. He got a phone call in the middle of this so he stopped paying attention to me and was focused on whomever was on the other line.

When he hung up I said to him "My job is to protect you in the media. If you don't let me do my job neither of us will *have* a job." Then he grimaced and begrudgingly gave me an angry but silent thumbs up. His jugular popped out again. When we got to the airport he stormed out of the car so I did what any normal Southern girl would do: I got out of the car and gave him a big bear hug.

I still don't know why I did that. Maybe I was trying to diffuse the situation. Maybe I was trying to show him *I* was the one in control at that moment. I was not losing my cool or displaying *any* fear of him. I was cool as a cucumber. Flummoxed, he didn't know what to do but he never messed with me ever again and from then on he trusted my judgment and never edited a word I wrote for him.

Despite the intermittent threats of firing (it changed weekly with which staffer was on his bad side), I was on Cloud Nine, living the dream, walking the halls of D.C. pinching myself, wondering if it was real. I remember walking past the Texas delegation on swearing in day after a night at The Monacle restaurant where all of us young staffers had raced on foot through the D.C. streets that evening to get to the party, a long line of us running in business suits in excitement, followed by way too much celebrating back at the condo, thinking "Wow, this is it. My childhood dream has come true!" The Texas delegation was blonde and beautiful and much younger than we were but we had gravitas, we had experience, we had a spitfire in office who wasn't afraid to take on a fight on camera. It was exciting! I had all the national TV shows on speed dial.

One time stands out in particular: Chris Matthews called my cell phone. The Chris Matthews, media star of MSNBC's "Hardball." For any political junkie like I was at the time, this was the Holy Grail of political show calls. I thought I was going to pass out. I remember glancing down at my cell phone and saying under my breath "Good Lord, Chris Matthews' show is calling me," not knowing it was actually Chris himself on the line:

"Hey, this is Chris Matthews. Is the Congressman available?"

Of course I was sitting at home on my couch after work and thought it was a prank call at first but eventually I patched the Congressman in from my phone and the three of us had a teleconference while I stood on the front stoop of my house so that my kids couldn't be overheard in the background. I felt so tapped into the national consciousness and, more importantly, I felt like I was making a difference with legislation pitches Massa would hear me out on. And I was standing outside in suburban America on a quiet, tree-lined street talking to freaking Chris Matthews and a United States Congressman. It was surreal and everything I'd ever dreamed about as a young girl. I was making a difference...

I felt like we were fighting the good fight.

Once Massa even asked me to sit at his desk in Congress and meet with constituents when he had to go vote on the House floor one time. I was reluctant to do so but he encouraged me to fill in for him because the constituents had driven all the way down from Rochester to Washington, D.C. but he couldn't miss this vote. I remember sitting down in the stately room and looking behind me to see the Capitol and thinking how honored I was in that moment. A little part of me wished I was the representative because when I was in fourth grade I had wanted to be President. Now that I'm older I do not wish that pain on anyone.

Despite Massa's idiosyncrasies and his sometimes bizarre statements, such as his assertion that he had superhuman senses of smell and hearing due to the cancer treatments he had to undergo years before (he actually said that on a drive to Ithaca one time), he could be gracious to staffers if they were on his good side that week. He walked me to my car at his house that first night and put my coat on me, taking care to notice the tag inside of it was Russian and asking me why I was wearing a Russian-made coat, to which I replied "Goodwill Store." It was then he realized I was not a privileged youngster like many in D.C. are. I worked my way up from nothing to be there and that earned respect from him.

He also listened to me recount my desire to escape my unhappy marriage as I was driving him to Ithaca from Corning one afternoon in October 2009. He had sympathy for my situation and asked pertinent questions and said he would do what he could to help me. I believed him too. I wasn't being physically abused at this point but the marriage was not working and Massa seemed to understand that well.

Another time early on in his tenure, my son with autism had run away from the group home for the first time and no one would give me answers. I was in the Southern Tier working, about three hours away from my son's group home, so for ten minutes we didn't know where my son was and if he was okay. When they finally retrieved him the staffers refused to give me the details. I was working with Massa that day and I told him what happened.

He said "Pull the car over." I did and he got out and began speaking tersely into the phone. He had called the group home and I don't know what he said to them but after that I got all the communication and information I needed for my son. I also got respect from the staffers.

That was the Massa I had gone to work for – a valiant fighter, a soldier for good who did not back down from a fight when his constituents were being wronged. It was sad to realize that interspersed with all of the good he was capable of dishing out he could also turn on a dime and bully people into doing things the way he wanted them to be done even if they were not the right things to be fighting for.

Months wore on and it was amazing. President Obama had blazed into office and had introduced the health care bill. The constituents across the country were on fire and I was in charge of all town hall meetings. The Democrat Congressional Campaign Committee had me on speed dial, asking weekly how the town hall meetings of the week had gone, sometimes calling me minutes after they were over.

Suddenly, all of these people I had grown up admiring on TV, Chris Matthews, George Stephanopoulos (whose show the Congressman was obsessed with getting on, to the point he called me on Christmas Eve demanding I get him booked on it), Steny Hoyer, Barbara Boxer, and so on were suddenly at events I was going to or were having their staffers call me. I felt I had joined in the league of helpers…I wanted to help and here this congressman was letting me help in a very direct way.

And then suddenly one day the mad reality came crashing in. Why does madness often accompany genius? I was so close to being able to move out and get a place for my children and me with Massa having agreed to give me a promotion and a nice raise and then suddenly I lost my job, again through no fault of my own, just like with the Governor Spitzer deal. Strike three for New York politicians, unless you count former Representative

Kuhl, which would make it Strike Four (Spitzer, Kuhl, Lee and now Massa). I was sick of these madmen.

I learned I had lost my job along with all of my colleagues when this politician, my boss, also resigned in a scandal...on national TV. "Tickle Me Massa" became a late-night TV show running joke but I knew the pain of what we staffers were going through. I wasn't privy to what went down to lead to this resignation (we had no warning this was about to happen) but I was privy to the aftermath. Because I mainly worked in Rochester, I didn't see how he was behaving in D.C. during the week.

So I learned I lost my job while driving down the road listening to the radio broadcast of the press conference. My phone began blowing up with every national news show I had been chasing for the congressman for nearly a year. "Inside Edition" was calling. "The Today Show" was calling. And yes, the much sought after "This Week With George Stephanopoulos" was finally calling.

All it took was a scandal...

All those months when I was calling them with actual ideas the congressman wanted to discuss to move our country forward had no interest from them since he was "only a freshman." I get that now but at the time the truth stung. They only wanted to talk to me now because of my access and proximity to a madman. Now it was my turn to turn them all down.

I was so distraught that I wasn't paying attention to how fast I was driving. I was crying so hard that it took me a few minutes to realize there was a sheriff's deputy behind me with his siren on and his lights flashing. I pulled over and continued crying. The officer tapped on the window and I rolled it down.

"Do you know how fast you were going?" the young man asked.

"No...." I blubbered, all Meg Ryan in "When Harry Met Sally"-like. "I just lost my job!" I wailed.

"What do you mean?" he asked, confused about my reply.

I turned on the radio a bit louder and said "Congressman Massa just resigned and I'm his press secretary. Listen."

"Hold on," he said and walked back to his car, looking kind of in disbelief. I could see him fumbling with the panel on his dashboard and then he began talking to someone on his handset.

A few minutes passed and then the officer came back to my car. "I'm going to escort you home," he said.

Then he stepped away from my car and put his arm up to stop the cars coming and waved me onto the road and pulled his car behind mine. I went home and crawled into bed and cried for days. (And in a life-is-stranger-than-fiction twist, this same officer would be one of the responders on the night I was attacked.)

After that I was done with politics for good.

"Too many madmen" I told everyone.

CHAPTER 8:
INCESSANT PROXIMITY

Eighteen months of unemployment followed the sudden and unexpected loss of my Congressional job because I couldn't relocate to Washington, D.C. from Rochester due to my kids being in school and locally no one would hire me because of the stigma of scandal or because I was, as they claimed, "overqualified." People would interview me for jobs just to get the dirt on the Congressman, something it took me a few interviews to realize was going on. Once they discovered I wasn't involved in the details that led to the resignation I was of no interest to them.

I had been the last staffer in the Rochester office to stay on, doing work that had no personal interest for me: answering phones, taking meetings with constituents about problems I had zero experience with but still trying to get answers for them nonetheless. I was reassigned to health care and border patrol questions on immigration due to how close we are to the Canadian border. I took meetings with folks trying to get their mother's legal citizenship from India and answered questions about the new health care bill. I was able to do the job well but my heart was no longer in it because I knew that come the November election a few months later, my job was over. Little by little the staffers moved away or found non-political work while I kept coming in and manning the fort, so to speak. By the end it was just me, the other two remaining staffers deciding to retire from working altogether due to their age.

On the last day, the day before the November election, I packed up my desk as I sat there alone in what was once a bustling office with a dozen staffers, the phones always ringing off the hook, my cell constantly buzzing from a reporter or from the congressman, my colleague Jared and I hammering out an excellent editorial or press release, interns flying about and the fax machine going strong. And now it was very, very quiet and empty. I walked around and looked at all the ghosts of the past haunting desks and locked all the doors and turned off all the lights.

Then I walked out the door of a childhood dream and said goodbye.

It was a very depressing time in my life, to have lost my dream job but also to have once again lost my way out to freedom from my very unhappy marriage, so I returned to gardening and running and working out. I thought if I made my body and mind stronger then I would find my way out of this mess. It was also a great distraction and running had always been a way to relieve stress and it kept me strong so I could handle my son with autism, who often ran away.

I worked my way up to running four miles a day and lifting weights every other day. I thought my physical conditioning would help me stay safe when my son lashed out with a tantrum but little did I know that conditioning would one day save my life...

I had been married to my spouse, a neuropsychologist, for twenty years by this point. We had four beautiful children, a big home with a white picket fence, and to all outside observers, we lived a lovely life. But the toll of my sudden unemployment hit us hard because I had become the breadwinner over the years.

At first I hadn't noticed his drinking because I was working so much. He hid the bottles before I got home. But once I was unemployed we were suddenly around each other more because he "worked" from home. It was an uneasy mingling, or as the writer Edna St. Vincent Millay so cleverly described long spent relationships, it was "an incessant proximity."

The reality of his sickness became apparent on the Massachusetts Turnpike in August 2011 but he would try to recover and smooth things over so it became this year of constant ups and downs with him.

Christmas 2011 was horrible. I had been unemployed for a year at this point and money was tight. I had a consulting gig but it didn't bring in steady money. He refused to go back to teaching or even try to find a job with a steady income.

To make matters worse, on Christmas Day he refused to wake up so the children could open their presents. Our children were little at this point, at ages when toys still have meaning to them. My son with autism was there and it was getting harder and harder to delay the celebration. My son cannot handle things changing or plans being canceled so I was starting to panic. When he acts out it can lead to chaos, escapes or physical tantrums.

Hours passed and my husband still wouldn't wake up. At first I let him sleep in because I knew it was a tough time of year for him. His father had died on Christmas Eve eleven years earlier but after so many hours had passed I realized he was going to sleep all day. If I had let the kids open the presents without him there would be hell to pay and I also wanted to do this as a family. Even with me being incredibly unhappy in my marriage for years, I was still a kind person who wanted the kids to have a semblance of an "intact" family. I also was still kind to him, my spouse, despite the fact that we were basically angry roommates by this point. In my opinion, a marriage is no longer a marriage when it gets to the roommates phase. It's just that – a legally sanctioned roommate. Who wants that? Not me, that's for sure.

Finally I got him to wake up and come downstairs so the kids could open their presents but he just slumped over in the middle of the living room floor and looked miserable. Photos of that day are too painful to look at because his misery is jumping out at observers. The kids were happy in them at least.

I tried in vain to get him to seek counseling and get on an anti-depressant but he refused to do so. He would lash out at me and project his issues onto me, saying that I was the one who needed counseling. When I asked him to join me in working out or running, he would scoff at me. He played basketball for a couple of hours on Sunday but it was just once a week and he'd come home and sit in his sweaty state for hours on the couch and then drink beer, thus negating the healthy effects of the pickup game.

The time of the game was also right in the middle of our children's weekend family outings so it left the care for all four children on me. I would ask him to move the game to a later time or an earlier time but he couldn't control it. Wednesday nights after his church group would have been perfect instead of Sundays from noon to 3PM, when I had all four kids at home eager to go and have some fun. Once he got home from the game he was exhausted so that he never went anywhere with us as a family on Sundays. I did it all alone and got used to it. That showed me that I could handle this life by myself.

His complete absence all day and night on Sundays led to some stress in our marriage. He accused me of being insensitive to his need for guy time but I told him I loved that he had guy time but why did it have to be during the most stressful and also meaningful time slot of our children's weekend? Our son with autism was home on the weekends and it was incredibly stressful for me without help. I wanted Sunday afternoons for family outings like I saw all the other families doing at farms or at the lakes. It was a disagreement that we never found a resolution for.

If I had an activity that took me away all day long from my children on the weekends I would find a different way or day to partake in that activity but he didn't care enough about the rest of his family to do that. He made us seem selfish for wanting to spend time with him and he could never see the irony in that.

A short time after Christmas 2011, I was awakened in the middle of the night by a commotion in our bedroom. Our daughter had an intense fear of the dark so we had finally, after years of trying every tactic we could find, moved a couch into our bedroom so she could sleep there and so the nightly struggle would just go away. I had grown tired of sleeping on the floor beside her bed holding her hand until she fell asleep and then quietly scooting out of the room. Usually she woke up the moment I got out of the room. Oftentimes she would end up in our bed when I did this if she didn't wake up as soon as I got out of the room. Some children have a greater fear of the dark than others and she was one of them. It was not so bad with my three sons, who adjusted to having to sleep in their own rooms much easier.

It was taking a toll on my body but also on the quality of our sleep and our marriage. The couch was a stop-gap measure until she either grew out of this years' long fear or until something else we tried worked. Nothing had worked over the years, despite specialists and tactics. It also didn't help that we were blamed for being ineffective parents by smug parents whose children were different than ours. It helps no one to be smug and to assume all children are the same or that parents are "doing it wrong." Every child is different and there is no one-size-fits-all method that works in anything in parenting.

When I sat up in bed that night I could see my big, tall, imposing husband standing over the couch leaning down with his right arm pulled back as if he was about to punch my little girl.

"Oh my GOD, What are you doing!?" I demanded.

"Mommy!" my daughter cried and I ran over to her and grabbed her and ran downstairs and locked us both in the guest room.

My husband followed us and spoke to me angrily through the door. I discovered that my daughter had pissed him off and he was tired of her back-talking him. She did this to me too on occasion but I didn't try to punch my child. His response was to threaten to punch a little girl, his daughter, in the stomach. I shudder to think of what would have happened had I not woken up.

(I would later learn that while I was at work on July 3rd, 2012 that my husband had been driving the three younger kids to the video store and our daughter had once again been smarting off to him and he said while driving "I am the Angel of Death and I can punch you in the stomach until you can't breathe!" in order to get her to shut up. It pains me to this day that she was so scared of him that she didn't tell me what he had said immediately or once I got home from work and before I took the kids to the lake for the Ring Of Fire celebration at Conesus Lake. It shows how used to the threats they had gotten and how they kept these threats from me. It also shows how successful he was in scaring them into silence and submission. It sickens me just thinking about this.)

I informed my husband that my daughter and I were moving into the guest room and that was that. I said something like "I have to get the two of you away from each other for a while. This will help us all get more sleep." So I framed it in a way that made it seem like I was helping him. I was clever in how I approached this. If I had made it about shaming him I'm sure he would have attacked us both at that moment, now that I have hindsight into his sickness.

I told a few friends about what was happening at home with him and the children and I consulted a medical professional but there was no evidence. It was my word against what I am sure would have been his well-delivered protests. After all, he had four degrees, one from the Ivy Leagues, one from the best writing program in the country and two from one of the best brain research universities in the world.

He had the pedigree, I had the pain.

And again, menacing is hard to prove. It was our word against his and he was very, very good at putting on a good public face, he with his Ivy League education and doctorate. I was just a petite Southern girl whom he could portray as an overprotective and emotional mother. This is where challenging cultural assumptions becomes so important. We have to check our bias at the communication opportunities, whether it's at the grocery store when a neighbor reaches out or at the church service, in the doctor's office or at the water cooler at work.

"Why didn't she just leave?" you may ask or think to yourself? It is a shaming thing to ask because it blames the person for their efforts to handle abuse in the best way they know how while they are in panic mode, being abused and traumatized. It incorrectly places the blame on the abused instead of on the abuser. We should instead be asking "Why did he just not abuse?" (I use the pronoun "he" here because it is the most statistically reported gender of abusers even though anyone, regardless of identity, can be an abuser.)

And there are so many reasons she doesn't "just leave." I'll give you a few (and I'll use the pronoun "she" here because it is the most statistically reported gender but domestic violence can happen to anyone regardless of identity and, again, it can be perpetrated by anyone as well):

- she didn't have anywhere else to go
- she didn't have a job or any money
- she had no one she could trust
- she couldn't get her kids out safely
- he knew where she worked
- he controlled all the finances
- he had threatened to kill her and the kids if she left
- he had systematically worn down her self-esteem over time
- he had isolated her from family or supports
- she was in love with him
- she was pregnant and vulnerable
- he would ruin her life
- she fears shared custody and leaving her kids alone with him

I wanted out and was trying desperately to afford a way to do so, safely with my children. I was alarmed by his increasingly angry behavior and was planning our escape constantly, brainstorming ways and hitting dead ends everywhere I turned. It was also hard to get anyone to believe the seriousness of my situation.

It's just that I had no job and nowhere to go, no family in the state and no one would help me. Because he hadn't hit me yet (ugh, what a sick thing to realize that we have to wait until a person is physically assaulted in most cases to have an actionable offense that leads to real safety for the abused), I had little I could charge him with. Menacing is hard to prove, remember?

(What I know now that I didn't know then is that it helps to have a history of 911 calls. However, I had been told if I called 911 "The first cop dies," which told me the children and I were already dead in that scenario. He was very good at threatening us, another reason the verbal abuse part of the Violence Against Woman Act is so important because if the verbal threats prevent her from being safe enough to call 911, there's no pattern of 911 calls.

It also helps to reach out early on to domestic violence shelters because they have access to resources and helpful information that I was trying to find on my own. A lot has changed and improved since I was attacked in 2012 so things are getting better for those seeking help out of domestic violence situations.

The culture is also changing and awareness is spreading. Fewer people are saying "I hope she gets counseling so that this won't happen to her again," which places the blame for being assaulted on the survivor and not where it belongs, on the person perpetrating the assault! Abusing someone is the abuser's issue. The abuser owns that action and the abuser is to blame for their actions. We have got to stop victim and survivor shaming and that starts by educating the public and the first responders and healthcare officials and law enforcement, and not just once but in an ongoing fashion.)

So from December 2011 until July 5th, 2012, my daughter and I slept in the guest room downstairs. I began basically living in the guest suite area of our big old house all day and night. I moved all my things out of the upstairs as well. The suite had a separate entrance to the outside, two separate bathrooms, a big mudroom that I decorated to look like a living room, a guest bedroom, a small attic that the kids decorated with artwork and pillows and chairs and used as a clubhouse, a laundry room and access to the garage and backyard, all without me ever having to enter the main area of our seven-bedroom house. I could come and go without anyone even knowing I was home. For the time being, it was perfect for our now rapidly crumbling marriage.

New Year's 2012 came and went with nothing eventful so I thought things had smoothed over, again. It's the long stretches of normalcy that make deciding on when to leave an unhappy but non-violent relationship so challenging.

"Is it bad enough to leave?" you'll ask yourself. "Stay together for the kids," people will say or the real kicker "In my day we just worked things out. People today are so quick to just split up a family instead of realizing marriage takes hard work."

All those things were said to me or running through my head. How do I "just work it out" if he's threatening to "kill us all"? Hmmm? I felt like I was harming my children for wanting out of a loveless marriage but staying together "for the kids" was also harming them emotionally. I was shamed into feeling selfish for daring to want to be loved, for wanting happiness in this one life we are granted. He hadn't hit us so was I being selfish?

Did it matter that during my pregnancy with our fourth child he had an affair? Did it matter that he never celebrated me on my birthday? Did it matter that he never helped out around the house or groomed himself? Did it matter that he wasn't really working so that we were spiraling into financial ruin? Did it matter that he was miserable to be around? To some people it didn't matter. All that mattered was keeping a family together.

Some people just love a good suffering. I'm not one of them.

So I was planning our escape. Despite all the guilt society spews with its lovey-dovey holiday movies and traditional family units on TV shows (both dramas and comedies) and family and friends lamenting the breakup of a "beautiful family" when I confided in them how unhappy I was, I was secretly and frantically looking for a job, any job by this point. There were few people I could trust enough to tell the full truth to though.

And I thought I had time…

Then around Valentine's Day in February 2012 he had another downward spiral. I was walking by the basement door one evening after dinner and he happened to be awake at the same time I was, a rarity in the last year of our marriage, when I noticed his eyes were very dilated. I didn't say a word but I just kept on walking past him, my heart racing because I knew he was high on something, which scared me. He went somewhere upstairs and I quickly gathered my children and put them in the car in the garage. I'd seen this before, back when we were in college, so I recognized that he was on some sort of mind-altering drug and I refused to let that be around my children. He also had this menacing look on his face and it scared the hell out of me. I'm so grateful I'm able to maintain a good game face and not show my disgust and fear when it appears in front of me because if I had, I'm certain he would have grabbed me at that very moment. We were only inches away from each other.

All those years of dealing with my son with autism's emergencies had conditioned me very well. I have an incredibly cool poker face and can maintain calm in incredibly stressful situations. One time in particular stands out:

We were trying a new medication for my son, a dissolvable, marshmallow-flavored anti-psychotic which had shown great promise for those on the autism spectrum. I'd filled the prescription and given it to my son and he took it well. Finally, a medicine that he didn't gag on!

So I locked it up in the "child-safe" portable medicine cabinet I had specially ordered and then locked the cabinet it was in and then locked the room it was stored in. A triple lock! I went upstairs to grab something or to check on my baby and was up there maybe five minutes. When I came downstairs the scene I saw horrified me. My son was sitting in the middle of the floor with dozens of opened packages of the dissolvable medicine strewn on the floor all around him. The so-called "child-safe" cabinet was opened and on its side on the floor beside of him.

I rushed over to him and saw that his mouth was stained with the remnants of the dissolvable yellow tablets and the entire box was empty. Panicked, I called 911 on my cell phone while I held my son in my arms. The 911 operator told me not to induce gagging because it may be a caustic substance but I told her I was holding the packets and none of them listed caustic substances. I didn't listen to her but instead went to my kitchen with my son still in my arms and pulled out a long-handled wooden spoon and called my doctor instead on the landline. I told him what had happened and that I wanted to induce gagging in my son to get it out of his stomach and he agreed. So I grabbed a gallon-size Ziploc bag and put the wooden spoon down my son's throat and caught all the vomit in the Ziploc bag.

At that moment the ambulance and EMTs showed up and we were all taken by ambulance to Strong Hospital where I handed the bag of vomit to the emergency room physicians. They just looked at me but I said "test it."

They gave my son charcoal to finish the emptying out of his stomach. They then told me they'd never seen a mother do that before, have the presence of mind to bring a bag of stomach contents to the emergency room, but they were glad I did because it got the medication out of my son's system quickly and it showed them how much he had ingested. It also likely saved his organs.

It remains one of my coolest under pressure moments. But at the time all I was thinking of was how to save my son. I trusted my instincts instead of what I was being told not to do by the 911 operator. I realize she was following protocol but I knew to trust my mother's instinct and my own research into the medication and my son was okay as a result. Afterward, I threw out the "child-safe" cabinet and never again gave my son enticingly flavored, dissolvable medications.

So incidents like that prepared me well for remaining calm in the face of shocking circumstances.

It was snowing terribly outside, a common occurrence for Western New York in February, and when I started the ignition to my car I noticed the gas gauge was on empty. My husband had a very inconsiderate habit of running out all the gas in my car, even in winter when it can damage the car, and he had done it again.

All throughout my pregnancy with our fourth child, who was the only one born in New York (the other three older children were born in sunny Southern California), my husband had left the driveway unplowed before he would leave for work. I'd be seven months pregnant and shoveling the snow out of the driveway so I could drive the other kids to pre-school or go to the store. A neighbor I hardly knew noticed this one day and began snow-blowing the driveway for me after that. Years later he would tell me he was so offended that a husband would allow his pregnant wife to shovel her own driveway that he did this for me without even asking. A stranger cared more for me and my well-being and for that of my unborn son than my own spouse did. So to even think my husband would refill my gas tank was a fruitless desire.

With me being unemployed I had no money to put gas in my car and my unemployment checks had run out. No one would hire me in my field so I began seeking jobs outside of my training. This was a hard sell in the economy in Rochester at the time but I was trying. To say I was depressed is an understatement. I was simply despondent and desperate.

Inside the cold car I weighed my options as my little children sat shivering in the dark night in the driveway. So I took off on the snow-covered roads very slowly driving around trying to find someone home. I hardly knew anyone in town as most of my friends lived on rural roads outside of town or out of state. I was also ashamed to admit that my happy home life was a façade. I didn't want to tell my friends and neighbors that my spouse was at home high on drugs. That would ruin my children's friendships and would isolate us even further socially. No, I would handle this on my own, something I am so prone to do. Growing up the oldest child in a home with sporadic arguments led to me assuming the role of protector of my two younger siblings and it persisted into my adult life as a mother.

One time from my childhood in particular comes to mind that eerily mimics this night. My little sister came running into our shared bedroom on New Year's Day around 1990 or 1991. I was going to college at night and working sixty-hour weeks as a bookkeeper in a local grocery store to pay for my tuition and car payment and braces. I paid for everything in my life once I turned eighteen. The only perk I had was living at home while I did this since my apartment roommate had bailed on me and I could no longer afford it.

So I was living at home again and my parents' marriage was once again rocky. When I was four or five years old I'd seen one argument between them where a candy dish was thrown across the room. That night my young mother had grabbed my sister and me and whisked us away to Johnny's Motel in State Road, North Carolina. We stayed overnight one night and mom went back to my dad the next day. A few years later we passed by that motel and I commented to my mom "Hey, I remember that place! We stayed there one night when you and dad had a fight." My mom was surprised I remembered it but kids have a way of crystallizing shocking events in their mind, especially those that impact their survival.

The only other physical violence I ever witnessed between my parents happened when I was either a pre-teen or a teenager. I was washing the dishes at the kitchen sink, which overlooked the backyard. My folks were working in the yard, probably trimming branches along the edge of the woods of the state land that abutted our two-acre rural property, when all of a sudden they began arguing. The next thing I know they began fighting. Dad was pulling mom across the yard and she was screaming. I stopped washing the dishes and started to run outside to break it up but by the time I got to the door my dad came in the door with blood on his mouth and on his teeth.

"What happened?" I asked, scared. "She hit me" my dad said, kind of half-laughing, kind of dismayed. Then I saw my mom and she was scared too. "He dragged me across the yard and I taught him no one does that to me!" she said, or something along those lines. Somehow they diffused this argument but I don't remember how. I just remember thinking they shouldn't be married anymore and began regularly asking my mom to leave him. She never did though, at least not while I was still living at home. "Stay together for the kids" you know...

Years would pass until New Year's Day 1990 or 1991. When my sister came running into the room she said "Mom and dad are fighting." I stuck my head out into the hallway and could see the profile of my dad sitting in a chair in the living room. He had a shotgun resting on the floor between his legs, the barrel touching his chin. I quickly ducked back into our bedroom.

"We have to get Corey!" I said to her. The problem was that Corey, our little brother who was probably eleven years old, maybe twelve at the time, had his bedroom right beside the living room and the only doors out of the house were through the living room, right in front of where my dad was sitting with the shotgun to his chin. I stood there thinking for a few seconds before deciding what I was going to do. I could not let my little brother get hurt and I was not leaving the house without him.

So I made a decision.

"Let's go!" I whispered quietly as I grabbed my car keys, my purse and my little sister's hand. She was around fourteen or fifteen years old and not driving yet. As we quickly tiptoed down the hallway we ducked into our little brother's room and grabbed his hand and dragged him into the living room past my parents as fast as we could without saying a word.

My mom was standing in front of my dad with her hands on her hips and didn't take her eyes off of him as we ran past. My dad was crying and staring at my mom. In my mind he was about to kill himself or kill us all. The look on my mom's face was like "Really?" She didn't seem to believe him but we sure did.

I quickly loaded my little brother and sister in the car (this was before cell phones) and raced to my grandmother's house about ten minutes away. She was my dad's mother and she had this calm, Cherokee demeanor about her. She was stoic but firm and had great command over her family. I knew she was the only one who could help us.

I told her what was going on and she drove to my house while I took my siblings over to my Uncle Roger's house for the night. After a while the phone rang and my grandmother said all was okay and the shotgun wasn't loaded. My mom had told my dad she wanted to leave him and he had threatened to kill himself. My mom had known the shotgun wasn't loaded but my brother and sister and I hadn't known this.

After that I begged my mother to get a divorce more often and more emphatically than before. "We can't live like this" I said. She said she knew it but she couldn't find a way out. I'm not sure why. She lived near her family but they weren't that close in retrospect. I also think she was embarrassed. What I do know is that after that I began planning on moving out. I wanted my brother and sister to move out too but they were minors and I couldn't control them. It never occurred to me that I should call 911.

I had never heard the term "domestic violence" back then. We handled things within families back then. We just "worked it out."

So this upbringing informed the way my mind worked. Keep it together, stay calm and handle it yourself. Sadly, it's a very common way of thinking and living that can be found in all echelons of society. It's also why domestic violence can be so deadly in less-informed cultures. If law enforcement doesn't know about it they can't do anything to help.

It's also how what was happening in my marriage didn't seem as bad as what I had grown up around. My spouse didn't have any weapons that I knew of. He and I had never had a dragging fist fight (yet). We had a lot of good times interspersed with the bad, unlike most of my parent's marriage.

Yet here I was with my kids in the cold February night not knowing what to do or where to go, thinking I could handle it myself. I drove around until the car was nearly on empty, knowing at home my husband was high on something. I pulled into the nearby gas station, a family-owned supermarket/gas station setup, and sat there thinking under the store's parking lot lamps. Snow was really covering the ground and roads now. Where were the snow plows? The one friend I did trust nearby wasn't answering their phone and the only other one I trusted lived way across town down very rural (and surely unplowed) roads.

The children asked me where we were going. I had driven by my good friends' house again but they weren't home and they still weren't answering their phone. My cell phone had only a few bars of charge left. I was getting desperate. We couldn't stay outside, it was way too cold, and I was running out of gas and phone charge and I had no way of getting any more money or gas. The kids were complaining "Mommy, we're hungry! When are we going to eat? Where are we going? What's wrong?"

I was so desperate…I looked up in the rearview mirror and saw their beautiful but worried faces. "Stay together for the kids…"

So I dialed my husband on his cell phone.

"You have to get help. The children and I have left and we're not coming back unless you agree to get help tomorrow first thing" I said firmly.

He began crying. "Okay," he cried. "I promise. Just come back home."

I reached into my purse and pulled out my hunting knife. When I worked in Congress, the District Director, Dave Marion, had sent me to represent the Congressman at a sportsmen's conference at Roberts Wesleyan College and Pearce Memorial Church in North Chili, New York since it was a few miles from my house at the time. The first year I had gone in a skirt suit and knee-high boots and was laughed out of the place. I had thought you represent the Congressman in business attire at all events. I was wrong. At sportsmen's conferences you dress the part of a sportsmen's, or woman in my case.

So the next year I had gone in prepared. I wore jeans and a flannel shirt and got connected to all these hunters. I had grown up with hunters and had even gone with them a few times but I had never had a real interest in hunting. But to prove I could hang out with the big boys at this conference, I dove into an archery demonstration and before I knew it I was practicing archery and obtaining my hunting license for both bow and rifle. I went hunting with a group of them and found I enjoyed being out in the woods in the quiet mornings and early pre-dark evenings. I'd take my journal and sit up in the stands and write and take photos. There was very little actual hunting but I didn't care. I saw the deer and other wildlife and that was enough for me. Once I saw a fox in the moonlight and it saw me. We stared at each other for what felt like several minutes before he trudged off in the snow. I was on my way home because it was dark and the hunting time was over but that evening walk remains one of the most lovely experiences I've ever had in the woods.

During that time I obtained a series of weapons for hunting, mostly at the encouragement of my new hunting acquaintances, including a few big knives and a little pocket folding knife they gave me, which I now had in my purse and carried with me for protection when I jogged.

I unfolded the knife, a little three-or-four-inch silver Kershaw Chive model that fit into the palm of my hand it was so small, and let the sharp blade lie parallel with the forefinger of my right hand. If I was going to go back inside the house with my chemically altered husband, who at this point had not physically harmed us so I still thought I had no actionable offenses to report to the cops, I was going in armed to protect myself and my children. A small part of me thought I was overreacting but I like to be prepared. (And this is where society needs to stop making claims that women are "emotional" and "overreacting" when we report abuse because that perception stops us from trusting our gut instincts and we under report.)

The kids didn't know what was going on. They just thought we were having a strange wintry car ride. We pulled back into the driveway, the snow so deep and the roads almost unmanageable by this point, and I got the kids out. I could see the glow of the house lights from the driveway. He was in the music room just off the living room.

Slowly with my three younger kids hanging onto me (my oldest son who has autism was at his group home by this time), we cautiously entered the house. The knife was hidden in my palm, my keys in my left hand. I remember standing in the mudroom with my kids, nervously trying to decide if I should keep moving forward through the house or if I should turn back and go to the car. I felt I had no options but to keep on going.

By this point the kids had picked up on my fear and were themselves afraid. They began clinging to me as we trudged slowly through the mudroom, down the long hallway connecting the guest suite to the rest of the house, down the hallway by the kitchen and to the right through the living room where we stopped against the couch across from the music room. It was about fifteen feet away from where my husband was.

I could see him laying across the love seat in the music room which is at an "L" angle adjoining the living room. I kept my distance while the kids clung to me. I let my forefinger run over the smooth edge of the knife that I was hiding in my hand to reassure myself I had protection.

He had been crying.

"Are you going to accept the help I find for you tomorrow?" I demanded.

"Yes!" he cried.

"Alright. The kids and I will stay here with you as long as you get counseling and start medication. If you don't do this then we are gone."

He agreed. Then the kids and I all slept in the guest suite and he slept upstairs. I locked the deadbolt on the guest room downstairs but I don't remember getting much sleep. The children now knew that something was very wrong in their parents' marriage.

CHAPTER 9:
GRADUALLY, THEN SUDDENLY

The next morning the first thing I did was call a local counselor who had previously been our marriage counselor when our fourth child was born years earlier. I told him what was going on and he referred me to a specialist. I set up the appointment for later that afternoon.

To my relief and surprise, my husband went to the appointment. I had told the counselor on the phone earlier that day the details of what was going on. I informed him that I didn't know what my husband was on but I suspected it was marijuana because when I first met him in college he was what I thought was a recreational or casual user. Many students I knew in college smoked pot at parties and I eventually got my spouse off of it with an ultimatum that I was going to divorce him if he didn't quit. I didn't like how it made him act.

Most people would just chill out and get the munchies but he would act insane. He'd get all silly and giggly but he would also get very manic. He would hallucinate and get out of control and couldn't sleep. I couldn't stand him while high and one night I told him it was either the pot or me. He chose me...or so I thought.

I now doubt he ever fully gave it up. Any time there was a conference out of town I'm now sure he partook of it. He once told me about some mushrooms he and a conference attendee consumed and his mother was home with us when he told us about this. I became very upset and said "You're a father now. How can you be so irresponsible?" His mother had gotten sad and left the room. She knew more of his history than I did and I truly wish she had told me then what I later found out she knew about his past. In her defense, he lashed out at her angrily a few times to the point that I think she too was afraid of him. He did not act like this when his father was alive, a man I truly loved and admired. I had hoped my spouse would be like his father when he grew up but he never did grow up, apparently. He certainly was nothing like his father, who was a pillar of his society.

Years later I learned my spouse had been a heavy smoker of pot in his early adolescence, from about age eleven through age fourteen. He began using it again his senior year at Cornell and that led to a mental breakdown, something I had been told was just a momentary depression and not the full-scale mental breakdown it was and which he and his family downplayed to me after our first split.

I feel so stupid now in retrospect for believing them and for taking him back once I left the first time. But hindsight is so much clearer and starker than when you're in the middle of things without full knowledge of what's going to happen next. Like a frog in slowly heating up water, you don't know you're boiling to death until it's too late. These things happen gradually, then suddenly.

What I was yearning for and had been for years was a divorce. I was unhappy ever since my youngest child was two years old. I'd been unhappy before that but it was manageable. But after my baby was two years old, my husband confessed that he'd had an affair the entire pregnancy. It was a form of payback for me leaving him when we had only been married three years.

I was devastated by this. We had gotten back together and had gone to counseling. I'd given him four beautiful children. I put my education and career on hold to care for my family. I'd fully dedicated my life to him. I was a great wife and a wonderful mother. I threw him birthday parties and made our home and garden lovely. I planned great dinner parties, vacations and made home-cooked, scrumptious meals for us nightly.

But I had dared to hurt the narcissist.

When I left him years before we ever had kids he had never fully forgiven me. The night he confessed to having an affair when our child was still in utero, he sat on our music room couch and told me that ever since we got back together in 1995 that he had planned on hurting me the same way I'd hurt him. He'd researched ways to do that and the only equivalent way he'd found was to have an affair while I was pregnant. He confessed this all to me that night in February 2005 when our baby was only two years old.

So his calculated and cold mind did just that – planned on revenge and payback.

What he didn't know is that by then I didn't give a damn. I had long ago stopped loving him and had never been "in love" with him. Oh, I convinced myself I was but when I was being honest with myself I realized I had made a huge mistake. I had married what I thought was my best friend but I never had that passionate physical desire for him that I'd had for other men I'd dated when I was single. When we broke up the first time before we had kids I had confessed this to him but he refused to believe it, saying instead "You're just confused." But I wasn't. I had just made a choice to marry smart instead of romantic.

I thought he was a safe choice. How ironic. I thought he was the smartest and most likely to bring about a stable and successful future. In my defense, at the time he was sane and had a lot going for him.

He was good on paper.

What he wasn't good on was pot. It made him crazy and I hated it. I hated him. However, I still wanted the father of my children to get the help he so desperately needed. Once I got him stable, I was leaving. Hell, I was leaving as soon as I got a job, regardless of how he was. I was so over letting this man suck the life force and happiness out of our lives.

But he knew it. Somehow he knew that the moment I got a job I was gone.

So he went to the counseling session in February 2012 but he treated it as Governor Spitzer had treated my friend Alex's legal challenge: an opportunity for debate and a determination to "win."

The counselor prescribed an anti-depressant which my husband gave to me to fill once he returned home from the session. I called our insurance and it wasn't covered but they did cover a generic form of it. So I filled it and gave it to my husband. He looked up the side effects and refused to take it.

"But it's the same thing basically," I said, exasperated.

"It has sexual side effects," he said.

I just looked at him in disbelief.

"We don't have sex," I stated, still in shock.

He just smiled at me in a threatening sort of way. It was then that I knew he was still sleeping around on me and now was not even trying to conceal it.

It explained a lot: his "conferences" and reckless spending, his newfound habit of heavy drinking, forgetting my birthday, telling me from his car in the driveway with the window rolled down "Oh yeah, your mom called. Your grandpa just died" and then driving off leaving me to collapse on the floor of the mudroom crying alone, flirting with women at parties right in front of me while I was seven months pregnant with our fourth child, bringing home pretty "babysitters" on a rotating basis.

The thing is I didn't care. I was disgusted by him. I hated him and wanted a divorce so he could screw whomever he wanted (and whatever fool would have his unkempt looking self) and I would have just laughed and handed him his things and locked the door.

So he refused the medication. The other non-generic brand cost more than $400 a prescription so there was no way we could afford that. This is a perfect example of outrageous medication costs literally risking lives, mine and my children's in this case.

I called the counselor to tell him this and to ask how it went. He said he couldn't share that information with me but that my assessment of my husband was accurate. He sounded pained on the phone with me, as if he wanted badly to warn me of something, but he couldn't divulge it due to privacy rules.

So I turned to my friends. I was a crying mess on the phone with one of them in particular. It was, however, very embarrassing and I was still trying to maintain some semblance of a normal family for the sake of my children and if I'm being honest, also for myself. At one point after a bad argument (he didn't care if he yelled at me in front of the kids or neighbors or friends or family or whomever) I asked the children if they would be okay if their mommy and daddy got divorced. "No, mommy!" they had all said. "We want our family to stay together."

I'd countered "But even if daddy is mean to us?" and they had all gotten sad and hung their heads down and said "Yes, we want our family to stay together, not like those kids at school whose parents are divorced." So that had resonated strongly within me. I want my children to be happy. At the time the violence hadn't happened so I thought it was just arguments I was facing.

Also, I had chosen this man and I had the white picket fence life. I'd already lost my dream job, did I really have to lose my dream life too? I could leave though, I really could, if I just had the money, if I just had someplace else to go…

(This is the reason that scene with Richard Gere in the movie "An Officer And A Gentleman" always makes me cry because I have been that person who has no place else to go. I've been the person who felt like nobody loves them.)

So I told my family and I told his family what he was doing. Everyone minimized it. No one would fully believe me. NO one thought I was in danger. I didn't think I was in real danger. We all just thought we were dealing with a depressed man on a certain course towards divorce. All I needed was a job…

CHAPTER 10:
CHRISTMAS IN JULY

With me being unemployed and tarnished by a national scandal, it was a seemingly impossible feat to find a decent paying job. I felt hopeless but I turned to healthy pursuits while seeking work, which for me was running, working out, writing and gardening. At one point I had forty-two rose bushes and over three hundred tulip bulbs. The day after the Congressman's resignation I planted an entire day lily bed. It was beautiful! I thought since my life was such an ugly mess I needed to literally plant some beauty. And so I did.

I also began a private consulting job and began writing again. A few stories I'd written about parenting were chosen for inclusion in an anthology on motherhood. There was a book signing and a party. Of course, my husband did not show up for it. He never could support me in my successes and was jealous of any achievements I made. He actively discouraged me from joining the newspaper's Editorial Board, which ended up changing my life for the better due to the friends and connections I made, and he disparaged my job in Congress, even laughing when I lost that job, our sole source of income. I had come home one afternoon and walked up the stairs by his home office and overheard him laughing about "Tickle Me Massa" and saying "Yeah that was the loser my wife worked for." After he got off the phone I stood there and said "Do you not realize that job was our livelihood?"

On my first 5K run, I crossed the finish line expecting to be hugged by him only to discover I was the only one with no one waiting for them at the finish line. How symbolic! He had left to go buy coffee from a shop owned by some young blonde he knew. It was quite demonstrative of how he had begun treating me in the last few years of our marriage. He could not celebrate me or any of my accomplishments. He was jealous of everything I did.

Eighteen desperate, sad and grueling months later I finally landed a great job with one of the connections I had made at the newspaper, (Alex Zapesochny's new startup), the place he had mocked me for writing at because it was unpaid, not realizing it was a great networking opportunity, and my freedom plan was coming together. However, somehow he sensed it. Maybe that's the real reason he mocked me for "working for free," as he often chided it, at the paper and later on for the two Congressional campaigns. But I trusted my instincts and followed my passions and it paid off very nicely.

Meanwhile, finances were tight and only getting tighter because I was the only one seeking work and our refrigerator had died. It was a hot summer and we were going to the store daily to buy ice and put it in the mini-fridge we had bought as a stop-gap measure until we could afford to either repair our main refrigerator or replace it. We were so broke by this point that we couldn't afford to replace broken appliances. He mumbled something about maybe being able to afford a deep freezer and put it in the basement for the meats (I was a vegetarian). I refused to invest what little money we had in a deep freezer since we eat mainly fresh foods and hardly any meat, other than the little that our small children consumed and his disgusting frozen burritos. That hardly warranted the need for a deep freezer.

So I axed that plan and I still remember the strange look he had on his face when he said we should get a deep freezer. It was the same look Governor Spitzer had had on his face when he asked Alex "So you wanna play lawyer?" It was confrontational, like challenge accepted. I remember thinking in the back of my mind that that was what serial killers did on those reality crime shows I liked to watch. I told myself I was watching way too many of those shows and was overreacting. Still, there was no way in hell I was letting him bring a deep freezer into our house. I think the only thing that stopped him from doing it anyway was not having the money to do so. He also hated that I watched those shows and seemed particularly bothered by it. I just like a good mystery and always have.

It is worth noting that a few years prior to this his maternal uncle had killed a family in Virginia and had been executed for the crime. At first we didn't believe he had done it but after the state presented its evidence it was apparent to us all that he was mentally ill and guilty. I had met this particular uncle at a family reunion and he had given me the willies even then. He had been angry at his son for sharing his French fries with me after an evening of playing tennis together. "She can get her own fries!" he had said angrily and I remember thinking how much hatred he had for women. Little did I know then how right my assessment of this man was.

One day shortly after the deep freezer debate and before I got my pay check from my new job, he brought home a huge gray plastic bin, the solid material kind you cannot see through, claiming it was to store the Christmas tree. I noticed it was big enough to store a body.

It was also July.

Alarmed, I began hiding car keys and telling neighbors and friends about his erratic behavior. That was also the same time that I called what was then "Safe Journey" (and which is now Resolve) and they helped me outline a safety plan, which included telling my neighbors and trusted friends in case of emergency, informing my boss since work parking lots are the number one place people are murdered by angry intimate partners, packing the "go bags" in my car for the kids and myself, hiding important papers off-site, and finding a safe house. They also told me to leave immediately if I could but they had no shelter. I hung up the phone with sadness because information is great but still I had no place else to go. Besides, I didn't want to be in a shelter with my kids anyway, we had no place for our pets, and so in my stressed out, desperate mind I had nowhere to go.

My husband by this point (and I hate using the word "my" when referring to him because I don't like to associate any kinship with this person but it helps to keep the story clear) was stealing my pay checks the moment I got them so I announced to him just days earlier that I was going to get a separate checking account since he spent all the money the first day I got it and he couldn't tell me what he spent it on. I realize now I shouldn't have announced this to him but at the time I didn't know what fresh hell was coming my way. I still thought I was dealing with a grownup, or at least a mildly grownup man. Cue the imagery of the frog in ever so slowly heating up water...

He also began hovering around the kids so that I was never alone with them to actually get them away from him and to safety.

Then the yelling began to intensify. What had been a stir up every few months had now become a daily thing in the last few weeks of our marriage. He was so angry people in town would see him and cross the street to walk on the other side of the sidewalk (something that was not shared with me until after the events of July 5th, 2012 because people try to be kind and let us keep up our illusions of being just like everyone else).

Anyone within five houses of us could hear him screaming at me and the kids but no one ever did anything. They didn't intervene or call 911. They let us have our privacy and I suspect they were also scared of him. I was. He is big and imposing and I don't blame them for staying safe. (After the attack people would approach me and tell me they heard him yelling at me but they didn't want to impose on our marriage. I get that. I now try to help educate society about what we can do and safely. Calling 911 is what people can do to help establish a pattern and a history for the address. There is no need for anyone to apologize to me about not calling 911 because none of us knew what was going to happen and the education around domestic violence was and is still developing into safer protocols.)

During this time he also accused me of having an affair with my new boss, something he regularly did whenever I worked with or talked to any man. I realize now this was classic projection since he was having multiple affairs (thank God I no longer slept with him and was therefore not subjected to STDs).

Things were rapidly deteriorating our last week of marriage, so fast that I was having a hard time reacting to keep it all together while working and keeping my kids under some semblance of normalcy. I watched in horror one afternoon as he took the bills from the mail I brought home from the post office and threw them away unopened in a very ceremonial and happy way as he stood over the trash can. I asked him what he was doing and he said in aggressive, feigned happiness "It doesn't matter!"

Suddenly I realized he was suicidal and amped up my escape plans. I was getting excited about our exit from this madman. (When I read this or remember these things in retrospect, I want to scream at myself "Leave now! Go now! Don't announce anything, just go! Grab the kids and go!" But I was that frog in the slowly boiling water not realizing I was being cooked alive…)

I also remember him delaying doing the taxes so that I had to force him to do them and sign them right in front of me. It was a mistake to leave them alone with him for a second though because he exchanged the forms I'd filled out and filed an extension instead, so when I mailed what I thought were our taxes, I was mailing the extension instead, something I'd just found out about and was angry with him over. It made no sense! We were owed money back so I couldn't figure out why he wouldn't want to file our taxes. I asked him why and he said "That's how they find you! You worked in Congress and I read that is how the crazies find you."

"Oh...my...GOD!" I thought as he said this. Cue the movie "Psycho" music from the shower scene with Janet Leigh. I just could not believe how far this once brilliant and promising man had fallen. Here was a guy who got a perfect score on the SAT and missed one on his GRE. Here was a guy who had four reputable college degrees who could sit and watch the game show "Jeopardy!" and know all of the answers. And yet he thought "they" were going to find us...

This gave me more urgency to speed up my exit plan but I was running out of time, which I didn't know back then. I kept thinking "Okay, today I will get a separate checking account, save up for about two or three months until I have enough for a deposit on an apartment, and then we'll move out." My mind works in To Do lists in a methodical, planning way. I thought we would have a peaceful breakup like we did back in college when I was in my mid-twenties.

But I discounted the heavier loss he would feel this time.

No longer were we divvying up the Riverside Shakespeare and The Beatles' "White Album." Now we were dividing up a house and a family with four children and he was having no part of that. Instead of two cats to share custody of, he had amassed in the last few weeks of our marriage a shocking sixteen cats! When one of my beloved cats had died (we had three at the time), he brought home a new cat without asking me. I was still grieving the loss of my sixteen-year-old cat, Sunday, and didn't want any new cats but he did this to help me he said. My protests didn't matter.

And then the next week he brought home two more kittens and then the week after that a third new kitten so that suddenly we had six cats in the house. Then they bred, of course. Then they had another litter. I was going crazy. Not only were my allergies in overdrive from sixteen cats (!) but he was refusing to neuter them and refusing to give any of them up for adoption. When I asked him what in hell he was trying to do he said "They're my lieutenants!"

I was now *living* with a madman.

I was also trying to take away his beloved cats in addition to his beloved children and home and so in his mind I was the offending party. Never mind that he wasn't truly working or cleaning or watching the kids or grooming himself. Never mind that I was fully supporting everything in our family. No. None of that mattered.

In his very sick mind I was to be erased.

CHAPTER 11:
THE DJIN OF INIQUITY

I was frantically trying to find a way out of my crazy marriage and a safe place to stay for me and my children, trying to save up money and start a new life of freedom. I told my new boss, Jay Baker, what was going on and didn't know how he would respond but that that point I was so desperate I didn't care. He hardly knew me because I'd only started my job on May 1st and here it was July 2nd.

It was a Monday and I had alluded to some marital troubles earlier and he had patiently listened to me. When I began to trust him a bit more because I was obviously showing up to work crying, he began helping me out by letting me work flex hours so that I could be home with the kids more. He also told me about some resources his church had shared with him, something that would be very helpful a few weeks later. And for weeks he let me spend the first few minutes of most work days in his office just crying and sharing what was happening to me. He helped me find a counselor and most importantly, he helped me find a safe space to vent and assured me my job was safe. Few people have such a blessing and I am forever grateful for him and the company I worked for.

I began to dread going home or being anywhere near him. I was living the classic "walking on eggshells" life. The kids got used to scattering away to another place in the big old house whenever he erupted with his volcanic rage. But still, menacing is hard to prove...

One evening my husband and I got into yet another argument (and it's important to note that I was not trying to do anything to set this man off as I am not an argumentative type and was actually trying to avoid him as much as possible but he kept seeking me out to threaten and chastise during the last few weeks of our marriage) and when I tried to walk away as I always did when his verbal abuse began, he blurted out "You're a djin! You're a djin! You're a djin!"

Well, I had no idea what a "djin" was and didn't even know how to spell it. I mentioned it to my boss the next day and his eyes lit up. He told me a "djin" is a Muslim genie and it was a derogative term for an immoral person. He felt that I was now in danger and I agreed. Given the other religious insanity my husband had been spewing out about him being God and the cats being his lieutenants, we both felt in my husband's mind there was a Holy War going on and I was the sinner to be vanquished. We put together a safety plan for work.

I would only later learn that my husband had been telling his friends and colleagues I was a djin, an imposter and a wraith along with shocking statements such as "the real Jerri left years ago."

Astonishingly, none of them thought to share that disturbing information with me. In his sick mind, when I had left him for failing to be an actual spouse back before we had kids, the woman who had come back to him to give him another chance and to give our marriage another try was an imposter. I cannot believe how many years he lived with this delusion and none of us knew it, not me nor his family nor his doctor.

It's possible the delusion came and went with stress. His ego was so fragile so when things were going poorly between us, perhaps he preserved his self-worth by saying to himself that I was a "djin" or imposter and when things were going well and he felt I was being a good spouse, maybe he let go of the delusion as long as my behavior fit his acceptance levels. I'll never know but I highly doubt he has ever thought of me since then as the "real" Jerri. I've rejected him and in his sick way of thinking back then, anyone in his opinion who would reject him must be an imposter. Never mind the abusive actions that led to the rejection.

I suspect it is the same sort of insane thinking and crazy statement that he had told the counselor I had gotten for him shortly before the incidents on July 4th and 5th, 2012. I have often wondered if that therapist should have told me this since it would have indicated I was in imminent danger. I suppose it would have been impossible for him to have known what was going to happen and so it must be a struggle for counselors to ascertain when to preserve patient confidentiality and when to warn others of impending harm. Again, menacing is hard to prove...

Later on I would contact Dr. Arturo Silva, the expert on Capgras Delusional Disorder, a psychological condition wherein a person believes that a significant other, such as a parent or a spouse, is an imposter upon seeing them. Strangely, in the condition, if the affected person only hears the person on the phone, they do believe they are the real person but if they see them, they think they are an imposter, leading some to speculate it is a visual processing disorder. I asked for articles from Dr. Silva and he sent me pertinent research papers to read and study. After back and forth correspondence and phone calls, together we came to the conclusion that my now ex-husband could suffer from this disorder.

However, I also found a few books about this condition in my husband's study and, while they could have been part of his professional study, (he does have a Ph.D. in Cognitive Neuroscience from UCLA where Dr. Silva also has an association, after all), he was not a therapist and did not hold a counseling certificate. So why would he need these books?

It seems to me his interest in Capgras Delusional Disorder was either because he suspected he suffered from it (he has always had an uncanny insight into his own conditions, which he then chooses to ignore or downplay) or he was attempting to set up an excuse for harming me should he have been successful. It's also possible he was having a justification war with his psyche to justify the harm he was planning to inflict on me. If he was killing an imposter, a Muslim genie or djin no less, then he was killing an evil spirit instead of the loving mother of his four beautiful children. The mind of madmen is a tangled jungle.

I remember discussing this possibility with the D.A. in my case, the wonderful Bill Gargan, head of the Monroe County District Attorney's Domestic Violence Bureau, and he said something like "I can't figure out if he's crazy or crazy like a fox." That remains the question we'll never have the answer to I suppose. I just know I don't want to be in any proximity to his particular brand of crazy. (Thanks to the awesome job that Bill Gargan did with my case, I don't have to be anywhere near my ex-husband, and for that I am forever grateful.)

What I *also* know is that under duress, seemingly sane people can act crazy. We see it in the news all the time. "He just snapped," people will say after yet another gun rampage or "She seemed fine the last time I saw her" after another suicide makes the news. And yet my husband didn't "just snap." He melted down over the course of a year in what was at first short bursts of anger followed by weeks or even months of relative calm, only to start the cycle again so that I never knew which husband I was coming home to.

It was the very same feeling I had when I worked for Eric Massa. Was he going to be angry when I saw him or relatively happy? The mercurial temper and the uncertainty did their job well, which was to instill fear in those around them. It is the unpredictability of madmen that help them continue abusing for so long because they wax and wane, with periods of relative calm and assurance followed by punctuated bursts of cruelty or instability.

I dove into the research of violence and madness after the events of July 4th and 5th, 2012 and have come to the conclusion that Capgras Delusional Disorder is a form of ego preservation, at least in the ex-husband's case. Faced with the total rejection of him by me, his wife of twenty years, a woman whom he had met at age nineteen and who was at once his biggest cheerleader and defender, a woman whose accomplishments he once took credit for (and which made me so frustrated), he either had to accept defeat and loss again or he could project the failure onto me by making me an imposter. His narcissistic mind chose the latter for self-preservation reasons. This is the best guess I have as to the violent events that unexpectedly unfolded on the night of July 4th and the early morning hours of July 5th, 2012.

And so he deemed me a "djin," a Muslim genie whom he attributed all sorts of negativity to and with whom he was having a Holy War with in his mentally ill mind. It was literally a battle for life or death.

CHAPTER 12:
MY PERSONAL INDEPENDENCE DAY

I went home after work that Monday, July 2nd, 2012, and walked over to the next door neighbors' house before going inside my home. I barely knew the Brosius family as they kept mainly to themselves as one so often hears on the news. I sat down at their kitchen table and shared with them everything the children and I had been going through and how we were trying to get away safely. They were shocked but they also knew some of it because of how close our houses were. They'd heard the yelling and seen him arguing with me in our back yard and on the back porch.

Once when he yelled at me, I recall they were all out trying to enjoy time on their patio as a family with friends while we were on our screened in porch a few yards away. I begged my husband to please stop it but he refused. He just continued to yell at me so the neighbors got up and went inside. Since I hardly knew them even though we had lived next door to each other for eleven years, I just kept up the facade and ignored the angry elephant in the room, or in this case, in the neighborhood, just like they did. We all let me keep living in my pretend world of "everything is fine." We'd run into each other out in our yards and wave across the fence but that was about it. Once our kids were invited to go swim in their pool and once one of them helped me set up an air conditioner in my window but we all mainly minded our own business. It seems to be a northern thing unlike the more neighborly South where I'm from.

This fed into my mindset that this wasn't so bad. If it were bad, surely someone would call the cops. I doubt they knew that if I called the cops I had been threatened with death by implication.

I asked them that afternoon if they ever heard any future arguments to please call 911 first before offering any help. I told them what I was planning to do and what my schedule was at work. They had four older kids at home they said they would also share this information with, kids who were in their early twenties. I thanked them and went home and began planning the escape. It felt good to have my neighbors on my side. (I didn't know then how close I would become to this family but it is one of the nicest things that has arisen out of this tragedy.)

Once inside my home, first I packed the "go bags" and hid them under the fabric in the hatch of my car, one for me and one for each of my kids. I worked quickly and quietly because I knew at any moment he could venture downstairs and catch me doing this. Then I hid an extra set of car keys in the house and gave a set of house keys to a close friend. Things were getting real!

I called some friends my husband didn't know about and asked them if it ever came down to it would they let us hide out with them. To my relief I had many offers from friends all over to have a safe place for us all to stay. All these months of trying to handle it myself were wasted time. I did have a band of warriors on my side after all. I was not alone...

Finally, I told my boss what was going on and gave him my next of kin contacts should anything happen to me. I also contacted two close friends and asked them to be the guardians of my children should anything happen to me. It was morbid but in my mind I had to make sure my children would be well taken care of if he should actually kill me. It was a very real possibility in my mind, given the attempt to get a deep freezer and his recent purchase of a large gray opaque bin for the Christmas tree in July.

I was ready for a fight if it came down to it. In my mind at this point I knew there was a possibility of danger once he knew I was gone but I expected it to go down like this:

I would wake up early one morning later in the month, after I'd gotten my checking account changed to just my name and take the kids with me to a safe house while he was sleeping. The cats would be taken by the animal shelter at a later time. I wouldn't work in my office but would do so remotely from my safe house instead. The kids would switch schools and we'd all change our names. We would not buy a home or rent in my name so he couldn't find us. I would change my cell phone and car or at least have it painted and get new plates. I would go into hiding basically. That is how I envisioned this plan.

(I know it sounds like something from a movie but things in my life were like the movies during this time. I had an in-law who had murdered a family in Virginia, a boss who had melted down on national TV and who had espoused conspiracy theories to Esquire Magazine that involved Vice President Dick Cheney, and a husband who called me an imposter and viewed his sixteen cats as lieutenants. My real life was much stranger than any fiction I'd ever read.)

What I know now is that it was too elaborate a plan. What I needed to do was just leave and leave immediately. However, when you're in the thick of something so overwhelming, you can't see as clearly as you can in retrospect. I was ill-informed. I was that frog in the slowly boiling pot of water. Again, no one thought he would do what he did…

It was Tuesday was July 3rd, 2012 and I had to work. I hated leaving my kids alone with this man but I also was the sole source of income for them. To my knowledge he wasn't hurting them or yelling at them. That abuse was reserved for me. Later on I learned of some troubling behaviors the kids had kept from me.

After work the kids and I headed down to the annual celebration called "Ring Of Fire" at Conesus Lake. My husband never enjoyed it so I didn't take him with me. My daughter's best friend's father picked us up in his truck and I received an angry text from my husband accusing me of having an affair with this man. I assured him I wasn't and even if I did, how would I do so in front of my children and about 10,000 celebration attendees? Then I turned my phone off and enjoyed my family time. I was so over him ruining all the fun I tried to show my children.

We had a wonderful time at the lake. I remember staring out across the water and seeing all these red flares light up one by one and then the sky explode with beautiful fireworks thinking how this time the next year I would be free. Life had become so miserable on a daily basis, with the threats and the verbal outbursts and the financial ruin which he was causing, that I was on the verge of collapsing from all of it. So for that night I just wanted escape.

I took some great photos and dreamed of a new life. Little did I know how soon I was going to have one.

When we got back home it was around midnight so we went to sleep. I woke up on the Fourth of July, Independence Day, and to my surprise my husband was also awake. This never happened. He was a night owl and hardly ever woke up before 2PM in the last six or seven months of our marriage. I had such frustration with his hours because it basically left me with all the childcare and housework and meals while he was awake at night as we slept. It was such a selfish thing for him to do but I was also glad because I hated being anywhere near him in the end.

Around 10AM the doorbell rang. He ran to get it and there was a young girl standing there. He had invited her from the local coffee shop to come interview for a "job" he had.

"What job are you hiring for?" I asked incredulously, knowing that we had zero dollars and he had zero jobs.

"She's going to be my new media assistant," he said.

I looked at him like he was crazy, which he was, and just turned around and walked off because I now had zero f***s left to give.

I got ready for a trip to the store to buy 4th of July party supplies and was going to surprise the children with a cookout and fill up a little pool with water in the backyard for water balloons and wading. My son with autism was coming over for a mid-week holiday home visit so I had to get back before he arrived around lunch time.

I walked into the dining room to let him know I was going to the store and noticed now there were two females on the screened in porch sitting with him, one the "media assistant" and the other his "employee" who was often at our house doing some unexplained "work" for the past year or so. I was basically supporting her so I resented her presence in my house. He didn't bring in much money so I could not justify him having an "employee." She was nice but she was taking away money from my children in my mind.

As I was walking off I thought I heard him say quietly "Oh, that's not my wife. That's a wraith" in response to the new girl asking who I was.

"Did I just hear that?" I asked myself as I was rushing out the door to buy party supplies.

On the way to the store in Brockport, I broke down crying. I had finally hit the wall. In my mind I was thinking "My husband had just told two women I am a wraith. He is certifiably insane and I just want out! Please GOD let this be my Independence Day!"

I begged this over and over during the ten-minute ride to Brockport. In the parking lot I dried my tears and picked up the supplies. By the time I got back home about forty-five minutes later I had composed myself enough to fake being okay. I had gotten really good at pretending to be okay. Life had trained me well.

I grilled out the food and then sat in the sun on a lounge chair in the yard while the kids played in the water. I think I was reading Rolling Stone magazine while getting a little tan, listening to some good music and escaping a little and feeling like a teenager for just a little while.

When I had gotten home the girls (his "employees") were gone. He had gone upstairs into his office to do God knows what and I was enjoying being with the children. Suddenly he showed up in the backyard with no shirt on. He actually got into the kiddie pool with the kids and began splashing himself in it. This bothered the kids so they stopped playing and went inside to dry off and play video games.

I hid my face in a magazine and began reading. I noticed he was breathing heavily and thought maybe he was having a heart attack. A small part of me hoped he was. I feel guilty about that now that time has passed but it would have been such a much easier way out instead of enduring all this abuse. He ate like a teenager and rarely exercised, how could he still be alive? "Why do only the good die young?" I thought.

I looked up at him and saw that he was fine but acting strangely. He had gained so much weight I barely recognized him. He looked nothing like the tall, dark and fit man with so much promise I had married. The guy whose Ph.D. was from one of the best schools in the country (that I helped pay for) was now completely broke, looked like a homeless man, and was splashing off in a kiddie pool while breathing like he was a dragon. I couldn't wait to be divorced from him.

I got up and went to the screened in porch to finish watching "Gone With The Wind." I don't like having a TV on the porch but he did so I decided to go with it and watch a favorite film. At one point he joined me but didn't like it and left. It seemed like a pretty uneventful night.

After dinner it was time for our son with autism to be driven back to his group home. Since I found returning my son to the group home incredibly emotionally painful and since I had to work early the next day at my new job, my husband would be the one who drove him back while I was always the one who picked him up.

When our son was hospitalized for dangerous behaviors, it was always me who went to see him. From age nine until about thirteen, there were repeat hospitalizations. It was emotionally draining and often I had to sleep in the emergency intake on the fourth floor with my son until they found a room for him to get treatment. One of the first times he was hospitalized I slept there for a day and a half until they placed him in the Adolescent Psychiatric ward. He was there for an extended stay and I went to see him every day. My husband went once and found it too disturbing. As much as it slayed my heart to be there (because it is a very sad place), I put my own needs aside and went to see my boy.

My husband was unable to see life from another person's perspective I think. Or maybe his pain trumped everyone else's needs. Even when his beloved cat was dying a painful death, he couldn't be convinced it was time to end the suffering of the poor cat. Finally I said I would take the cat in and he refused and shocked me by stepping up to do it. When he got home he said he was unable to watch the sweet cat's face as he was dying. It reminded me of when our firstborn was getting circumcised. I had some stitches and was recovering so my husband had gone with our newborn. I called out to him "Don't leave him alone for a second. He needs to know he's loved." When he got back he said he took one look at the blade and left my son to be circumcised by the nurses while he stayed outside of the room. I was so upset by this.

So when our other two sons were born I was the one who went with them for the circumcision and I held their tiny newborn hands the entire time. And when our next cat died, I held her and watched her eyes as she transitioned into death. For me, it was painful and uncomfortable but I put their needs above my own discomfort. My husband wasn't able to do this. I'm puzzled as to why.

And ever since he had been in the group home, I was the one who called our son every night.

My husband never once called his son in the group home. It has been nearly ten years and he's never called his firstborn son.

He also oddly blamed me for our son's autism, saying that I should have given our son neurofeedback training even though he is the one with a neurofeedback business and degree, even though he is the one who has five other family members on the autism spectrum. Not that it's his fault because of genetics, which we cannot control, but how is this my fault? The logic is missing. Yet somehow it is my fault that I didn't "cure" our son. The degree of his ego preservation is amply demonstrated in this bit of knowledge.

Around 10PM on the night of July 4th, 2012 my husband arrived back home from dropping off our son, who was fourteen years old, at his group home. I was asleep in the guest room and my daughter, who normally slept in there with me, was at a friend's house for a sleepover. I'm so grateful for this because if she had been there with me I shudder to think of what could have happened to her. She's a spitfire and was thirteen years old at the time, teenaged and hormonal, and she no doubt would have gotten involved and gotten hurt or worse. My other boys, who were nine and eleven years old, were asleep in their rooms. It was a hot July night so they were barely clothed, the old house not having central air.

Suddenly there was a soft knock on the door. I could see my husband through the beveled glass top half of the otherwise wood-framed heavy door. It was an old house, built in 1906, so the doors and the whole house were made of sturdy and heavy, quality construction. The guest suite was a former examining room and waiting room because the house was owned by the town's former doctor back in the early days of the village. There was even a bell that dinged when you stepped on a certain part of the mudroom floor.

"Can I come in?" he asked. This was highly unusual. Typically he went straight upstairs to play on the computer after dropping our son off if I was already asleep. He sounded sweet and yet sad. At one time this man had been my best friend. We'd gone on at least ten cross-country road trips and had four beautiful children together. We'd seen forty-seven states together by road trip, had inside jokes and decades of history together. He had helped me get away from my troubled home life and seemed genuinely crazy about me in the early years (not textbook "crazy" but happy with me).

He'd helped me get into UCLA and find my first job with the university. He'd helped me move across country for an exciting new life. He'd shown me the fun of binge movie watching and the humor of Monty Python. He'd introduced me to incredible literature and the New England area, which I have grown to love.

And despite that history, by this point I hated him so much. I also remembered what he once was and that I once loved him like family. He *was* my family.

So I let him in the door…

At first it was fine. He asked if he could lie beside me and I took a deep breath and said "Okay." The light from the hallway was on and it filtered in through the beveled glass door, which he had shut behind him to keep the sixteen cats out because I am allergic to that many cats (who isn't?). I was having asthmatic attacks and I don't have asthma. I'd walk in the door to the house and couldn't breathe. We were having a discussion about how I had put up fliers and why no one was calling to adopt the cats.

I knew in my heart by this point that he just wasn't going to get rid of the cats but I didn't want to have this particular discussion so late at night. I just wanted to go to sleep so I could work the next day.

Then he asked if he could cuddle with me. Again, I reluctantly agreed but I could feel my body going tense. I asked him how it had been dropping off our son and he said it was fine but that on the way home he felt all alone in the world.

I asked him why he felt this way. He said something about seeing all the fireworks going off around the town after he had dropped our son off had made him feel like he was missing out on something. I had asked them all to go see the fireworks but no one wanted to this time since we'd just gone the night before without him (his choice).

I had heard him arguing with a colleague on the phone a day earlier and had listened to him recount all the ways he was getting revenge on the guy. He was energized and very proud of his plans. This was a common occurrence with my husband so I never knew just which enemy he was fighting and why. I found it childish, unattractive and exhausting. I suspected this was why he felt all alone in the world. No one wants to be around an angry, vindictive person.

But the truth is you are the architect of your own life. Where you are is based on choices you have made along the way. Where I was in life was based on the choice to marry a man I had only known fourteen months, a secret madman. While I didn't know his mental health history when I married him, I did marry him and I had to own that. I had to accept it.

But I didn't have to continue living with that choice.

No. This was going to be my Independence Day. I knew I was days away from leaving and I was excited about having freedom from tyranny, just like our founding fathers were in creating America.

"Can we make love?" he suddenly asked.

That was it. I could not *believe* he had the gall to ask me such a thing given that just a few days earlier he had picked me up and thrown me out of the mudroom door. Did he not remember also picking me up and throwing me out of the front door the week before that? Did he not remember screaming "The first cop dies!" when I told him I was going to call 911 after he threw me out on the street in my pajamas on a Sunday morning while the neighbors ducked inside leaving me alone and while my children were trapped in the house with him? Did he not remember only hours earlier telling his "employees" that I was a wraith?

Well this was one ghost that he wouldn't be seeing very much longer and it was certainly not one who was going to haunt his flesh or allow him to touch any essence of her spiritual plane or physical countenance. I had vowed the last time we had intimate contact that it would be the last time and I was keeping that promise to myself. The image of me crying in the shower, frantically trying to wash him off of me is so powerful and is one of the saddest memories I have of our twenty-year marriage. Contrast that with the happy face I had as I was walking down the aisle to join him in marriage...

I hesitated on my wedding day but why? What in my subconscious was I ignoring? I asked my mom about it and she said it was just wedding jitters so I let it go. Years later I now think that a part of me subconsciously could sense something wasn't right here. I wasn't that attracted to him though everyone else found him to be very handsome. So I walked up to him, said "I do" and tried so hard for many years. I think when the preacher said "in sickness and in health" that he didn't mean in dangerously violent mental sickness and health.

"We aren't getting along right now so I don't think that's a good idea," I said in response to him asking for intimate relations that hot Fourth of July in 2012.

Immediately, he angrily sprang up off the bed and yelled at me "You better watch it!" and then he stormed out of the room. It was sometime around 10:30 p.m.

I got up and locked the door and tried to go back to sleep.

Hours passed and then a little before or after 2AM I heard him leaving the house. When he returned after I called him back because I reminded him I had to work the next day and needed him home to watch the kids, all hell broke loose.

He began pacing back and forth past the guest room door and I realized I was locked in. The windows had been sealed shut somehow. Then he would go to the basement and I'd creep over to the door and unlock it and suddenly he would race up the stairs and I'd slam the door shut again. This happened a few times so I assumed he was somehow monitoring me, either from the creak of the floor boards, which were right above his head, or through some surveillance device. He is a tech whiz so nothing was out of consideration here.

Then he began demanding that I come out and prove to him that I was a woman, insisting that several females he knew had told them I was a man. He said I must prove to him I'm a woman over and over. I was so scared so I began dialing 911 again.

He asked me "Do you want a divorce?" and by this point I was so over him I just admitted the truth.

"Yes..." I said in resignation.

I looked up and saw him duck his head down and growl and then he broke the deadbolted door down. He came at me with such rapidity that I didn't know what was happening before I felt a punch to my face. I would later discover that right before he attacked me, he had been watching a battle scene in the movie "Little Big Man," starring Dustin Hoffman. It is a movie about many battles and one man's struggle, losing wives and children along the way, and it includes the line "Today is a good day to die."

When we first got together, it was one of the movies he insisted I watch to "catch up to him" in his entertainment vernacular. (He also made me watch The Twilight Zone, all the Star Trek series and shows such as M*A*S*H* and Taxi because I didn't watch much TV growing up and we didn't even have a family TV until I was in the fourth grade so I grew up playing outside in the warm South.) Television and film and literature, all fantasy entertainment, all fiction as opposed to non-fiction, were incredibly important to him. His Ph.D. was even on this genre as it related to attention spans as measured by brainwaves while watching film. So to say that fiction movies were important to his psyche is an understatement. He loves the escape of fantasy.

A few days after the attack I found the movie was paused on one of the battle scenes, leaving me to conclude he watched it for inspiration and had fully intended to kill us all that day and then kill himself or be killed by cops. I remember standing in his basement "man cave" a few days after he had tried to kill me and had kidnapped my sons and seeing this and being just horrified. The whole attack was so pre-planned...

You know how in cartoons they show a "Pow!" inside a star-shaped bubble? That's exactly how I saw the stars in my head when he hit me that night. I staggered backwards toward the bed and he grabbed me by the back of my head and slammed my face into the wooden chair beside the bed. I could see my blood was now all over the blonde-wood chair. He had flipped on the light when he broke the door down so that I could see his angry face as well.

At some point during what seemed like a very long battle, I was thrown onto the bed and he began trying to pull my pajama pants off . "Show me your pussy!" he angrily growled at me. "Prove to me you're a woman!" Can you imagine your spouse of twenty years suddenly screaming something so crazy to you?

He leaned over me as I was lying on the bed on my back and white foam was coming out of his angry mouth through gritted teeth. I don't remember saying anything but I was pushing him off of me with all my might. It is so strange to be having hand-to-hand combat with someone you've raised children with and have shared such special memories and events with. I never thought when I said "I do" in August twenty years earlier that things would end this way. I didn't think they would end, period. I had thought once I got married I'd stay married.

At some point I scrambled away from him and off the bed and I stood up. At one point in the fight I had reached under the bed and found an unloaded air rifle still in its box, a gift from Christmas time from a hunter friend. I swung it at him trying to hit him in the head with it like a club and I succeeded but he then grabbed it from me and slung it behind him so hard it broke the window at the foot of the bed.

The neighbor's son Tyler heard this as he relayed this later to me but didn't do anything, not knowing he should call 911. He was so used to us arguing, he said, that he thought it was just another argument. But this was way more than just another argument. It shows how we can become desensitized to violence, even in our own backyards.

After my husband broke the window with the gun in the box (I'm not sure he knew it was a gun in a box), I thought "This will get someone's attention. Someone will call 911. Help is on the way." But there was no help on the way…

So I punched my spouse in the face with my left hand and in doing so I cut my fingers over the wires he had used to hold his glasses together. It stung but I was so full of adrenaline I didn't care. I had never punched anyone before and didn't even know I had a left hook! It didn't deter him though and I was still standing and pleading with him to let me go, to let me show him on my phone that I was me by calling someone we both knew.

Instead he grabbed the phone from me and then leaned down and picked up my flashlight-filled tote bag from the night at the lake, a very heavy bag, and whacked me over the right side of my head with it. The world began swirling and I felt like I was going to pass out. I didn't know it then but he had just injured me pretty badly as my C4 and C5 vertebrae had just been compressed from the hit.

I remember making a groaning sound, a sound like I've never made before or since.

I tried to stagger out the door to my left but he threw me down on the floor. He had this vicious look on his face that was so determined. He looked around my head as if I had snakes swirling around me. I now know he was hallucinating from the K-2 bath salts he was on but at the time I just thought he was absolutely insane, which he was as well.

At first he was on top of me, again demanding I show him my pussy to prove I was a woman by trying to rape me. He pulled my pajama pants halfway down but I pulled them back up hastily. I was scratching him and punching him with all I had and I kept trying to kick him but he is twice my size.

And then he flipped me over. This was terrifying because I couldn't see him or what he was going to do next. For all I know he had his own gun or knife. I was face down on the cold tile floor and he began pressing himself into me. It was getting very hard to breathe and I remember thinking "So…this is it. This is how my life ends. This is how it all ends…" I was in shock and disbelief. This was wrong! This was not how my life was supposed to end. I was supposed to be an old lady who goes peacefully in her sleep after my kids are all grown and doing well.

I became so sad it is hard to describe. It was like a slowing down of time. There was a certain resignation, an almost acceptance within my mind and body, as if this was definitely happening and so I needed to make my peace with it.

I saw my beloved four children standing over me as I began fading out. I was being lowered into the ground in a coffin in my fading mind and they were looking down at me and crying. Then everything went black…

He had let go of me at some point in this struggle and when he did I regained awareness. I don't know how much time had passed. My heart exploded with adrenaline and I struggled around and got my feet under his chest and pushed with every bit of strength I had.

He went flying into the wall behind him and I scrambled to my feet. Because I had been hit so hard I was not moving in a straight line. I kept hitting walls but because I had earlier knocked his glasses off his face, he couldn't see me very clearly. He was also so high on chemicals that he had a hard time focusing I think. Every time he looked at me he not only looked at my face but at these invisible spaces around me that seemed to be moving based on how he kept looking at me. It was frightening.

He also was moving so fast, so strongly and so determinedly, like he was on speed. I was shocked with how quickly he had grabbed my phone from me, and then again how fast he got the gun away from me and finally with how fast he grabbed my heavy tote bag and slammed me on top of my head with it, as if it weighed nothing at all to him.

I managed to get to the mudroom door and frantically start unlocking all three locks, which we had due to having a son with autism who is an escape artist, but when I got to the third lock I felt him grab the back of my head. I was so scared because I thought I had finally gotten away only to feel him grabbing me so violently and jerking my head back so forcefully. Still, I kept unlocking the damn lock and managed to get it free but then he jerked my head back again so hard I felt something snap.

I jabbed him in the sternum and momentarily broke free. Again, I had never done anything like this before, had zero training in self-defense, so this was all pure survival instinct.

I made it to the door again at the top of the mudroom stairs and opened it.

Bam!

He hit me from behind and grabbed my right arm so tightly I thought he may have broken it. So I began fighting him again. I knocked him down on the middle of the cold tile mudroom stairs and stood up but he grabbed me again.

Again I began jabbing him as hard as I could with my elbow, over and over until he fell again.

Somehow he grabbed me and threw me hard down the remaining mudroom stairs. I sailed through the air and slammed hard into the bottom mudroom door and tore a piece of the wood frame off as I landed. It had at least a dozen glass pane panels in it so it's a wonder they didn't all break from the impact but I mainly hit the left corner near where the door opens.

I stood up and unlocked the wooden door and he grabbed me again. I could see freedom but he was holding me from it! I then used every bit of remaining strength I had and jabbed my elbow into his sternum over and over so hard he fell down on his ass and I opened the glass outer storm door and took off running for my life, literally.

All the years of being a runner to help me save my son with autism who runs away all the time were now helping me save my own life. So in a sense autism saved my life. I love the truth of that.

By this time it was around 3AM or so in the wee hours after the July 4th celebrations. Everyone had gone to the lake so not many people were home. I tried to scream but he had choked me so hard nothing came out. I looked back over my right shoulder and could see him squinting out at me. I knew he couldn't see me very well without his glasses so I put it in overdrive. It was the last time our eyes ever met.

I sometimes contrast that with the first time I ever met him back in North Carolina in 1989. The sun was behind his head and I couldn't make out his face as he stood in my apartment's doorway. At the time I didn't know he had a massive Messiah Complex so I joked that he looked like the Christ child with the sun behind him making a halo like that. At the time he had laughed so hard while he secretly must have loved it.

I also sometimes contrast it with walking down the aisle on our wedding day, how I never could have guessed that our first day as a couple and our last day as a couple would be so dramatically different.

He unexpectedly ran back up the stairs of the mudroom after I escaped the house so I used that opportunity to turn the corner and sneak into the side door of the neighbors' house, the same neighbors I had spoken to about the abuse on Monday just a few days earlier.

I began banging on the door like crazy, leaving blood all over it. After what seemed like forever, their son opened the door and quickly locked it behind me. Their four dogs began barking wildly and Tyler rushed me to a back bedroom and threw a dark-colored comforter over me.

"Call 911" I managed to rasp out. He did and then he got his dad, Dan, to wake up (how anyone could sleep through this is beyond me). Suddenly the dogs began barking wildly again.

My husband was at the side door trying to break in but the dogs thankfully scared him off. (I love those dogs so much! One of them is still alive all these years later, Maya, and I visit her often.) The neighbor's father looked out the window and said "He's left in his car."

I asked "Were my kids with him?" and he said he couldn't tell but that he was driving erratically on the sidewalks and not on the road.

I immediately went into panic mode and said "We've got to go after him. We've got to get my kids back!" but they wouldn't let me leave.

Then I assumed my husband had harmed my kids and they were in the house and needing CPR or some other form of rescue. The cops showed up and I raced outside and begged them to break into my now locked house.

I was barely clothed and bleeding pretty badly so I was taken to the ambulance which was now parked outside my house. The EMT cleaned me up but one of them spoke up and said evidence photos hadn't been taken yet. They said "Well let me just stop this spurting wound because she's losing blood." It was then that the adrenaline wore off a little and I could see I had cuts all over my body.

"I have to go" I said when the EMTs wanted to take me to the hospital. So they made me sign off on a form refusing transport to the emergency room and I jumped out of the ambulance and began begging the cops to help me get my sons, who in my mind could be in the house drowned in the tub or some other dangerous scenario.

I was desperate to get my boys back safely. There were two cops with me by now, one on either side of me. I was barefoot with only pajamas on and I was for some reason freezing. A neighbor brought me a blanket which I bled all over. I now know I was in shock from broken bones so the shaking was from that instead of cold air.

We approached the front of my house. It was probably around 4AM or so by now. I again begged the cops to help me break into my own house. "I have to save my boys!" I kept pleading. Even now, six years later writing this sentence, I tear up. I had no idea at this point if my kids were alive or dead. I felt guilty for escaping an attempt on my life. I was running to get help but was prevented from going back after the madman.

I had hoped to get the neighbors to help me fight him off and save my boys but it hadn't worked out that way. Now I didn't know where they were and if they were alive or not. In retrospect that decision probably saved my life but if I had survived and my boys had not I would have never forgiven myself. (Many times people will shame a woman who has escaped an attack but left her kids in the house. What they don't realize is you are trying to get to safety to find help to get the kids because you know you're too outweighed to save them by yourself, or they have the door blocked and a gun pointed at your head. Until you're in the situation you just don't know.)

My husband now had my house keys and my cell phone. We would later learn he also took my purse and slung my belongings along country roads all over the place, basically trying to erase my identity. (I never did get everything back but a jogger heard my phone alarm going off by the side of a rural road a few days later and picked it up. Somehow he figured out it was mine from numbers in the history and I at least had my contacts back. I got my purse back a few days later but it was empty.)

The cops said that the house could be booby trapped so they couldn't break in and I countered that he hadn't had time to do that. They said I didn't know how long he had been planning this and so he could have planned ahead. They refused to break in so I began to bend down to the ground and pick up a huge rock that I was going to use to break my own front window.

I almost had my hand on the rock when the radio of one of the cops announced "We've got him!"

I was so happy but I still didn't know if he had my boys and if they were okay.

"Are my boys with him? Are they okay?" I asked.

"Yes, we have the boys and they are alive and safe" the officer said.

It was the sound of my heart coming back to life…

After this glorious news, one of the cops walked me over to his car and took evidence photos of me. Then he had me to sit in the back of his car to take my statement while we waited on my boys to arrive from several towns over. My husband had taken my little boys on a high-speed police chase through the back roads between our village and several other towns before Bob Murphy of the Monroe County Sheriff's Office was able to catch him and grab my boys from the back seat while other officers pummeled my husband into submission and arrested him in Parma.

I was talking so fast from the adrenaline that the officer had to keep slowing me down. He was in the front seat and I was talking to him from the back. After I'd given him my statement he looked at me in the rearview mirror and said "You remind me of Jennifer Lopez in that movie "Enough."

I'd never heard of it nor seen the movie but he told me it was a very similar situation. By this point I was so relieved and exhausted. I knew my kids were safe and I had somehow come out of a vicious attack from a man twice my size and I was alive.

I looked at the officer through the rearview mirror and I said resolutely "He messed with the wrong girl..."

CHAPTER 13:
LOVE WINS. LOVE ALWAYS WINS.

"There is a land of the living and a land of the dead, and the bridge is love, the only survival, the only meaning." – Thornton Wilder, *The Bridge of San Luis Rey*

After I got my children back safely, we were handed black plastic trash bags and told we had five minutes to gather our things and get out. I had expected that my husband would be put in jail for attempted murder and that was that. But because he had access to money and there had been no previous calls to 911, it was likely he would be bailed out within the hour and free to come finish the murderous job he had set out to do just an hour earlier.

We were rushed to a secret safe house with the help of a neighbor who is a firefighter and the sheriff's deputies helped him move about five loads of our stuff to the safe house. That night after dark, my children and I sleeping on a friend's set of couches in their living room, our world completely destroyed, my middle son began to cry. "I want a new, better daddy!" he said. Then they all three started crying (my son with autism was safe in his group home and didn't yet know what had happened). I lay there assuring them everything was going to be okay and that I was enough for them. They fell asleep but I didn't. I wouldn't sleep much for the next several months, preferring instead to pace the house with a screwdriver firmly in my hand looking out the windows as I guarded my children.

Finally after about a week of living in the safe house, my folks came up to help me and take my kids to safety far away in case my husband was bailed out of jail. It was a very painful decision for me but I had to go to court a lot and I didn't feel the kids were safe if I wasn't with them in New York.

Unfortunately, my parents weren't able to give the kids the kind of comfort they needed so eleven days after the attack, with a broken nose, compressed C4 and C5 vertebrae and severe bruises all over my body, I drove the twelve or so hours to my folks' place in North Carolina and retrieved my kids. They ran to me like they hadn't seen me in years.

We would spend almost the entire summer hopping around from safe house to safe house before finally being assured their father, my husband of twenty years, my Ivy League-educated doctor, would be in jail for quite some time. So we moved back into our home and spent the next two years there while I tried to get our life back to some semblance of normalcy.

During this period we all developed PTSD. Any little noise would set us off. We cried a lot and we couldn't sleep. I continued carrying that screwdriver with me at all times. I became a multiple gun owner, despite the statistics that warn against this. I thought every strange man was him. Parking lots and parking structures scared the hell out of me. I hated nighttime.

And even though my kids and I eventually moved back into our home we couldn't sleep upstairs. Instead, for two years we camped out on a foldout couch in the living room and slept there. It was so cramped I could reach my hand out from the foldout couch bed in the music room and play the piano.

I had to endure a lot of physical pain and healing during this time. At work my hand would go numb if I wrote or typed too long. I continued traction on and off for a year to help alleviate the pressure. (Today the compression has spread to my C7 but my right hand no longer goes numb.) I had to learn to live with the geography of my face being permanently altered, something that took me years to accept. My children and I had to learn how to trust men again, something that took counseling and time.

My husband tried to win us back from jail at first. He tried denying the seriousness of what he had done before he finally accepted it and apologized. From jail he wrote some cryptically worded letters that frightened me and which caused me to request the Monroe County Sheriff's Office to monitor our house over the two years that the court cases played out. (The children had a separate legal case from mine and I had two cases as well so a lot of time was spent in court. I protected my kids from this and only I went to the court.)

During this harrowing two-year period, every little noise at night was, in our minds, him breaking in. The deputies would race over and come inside the house late at night while my children slept and use their flashlights to walk with me through every room of our big old house and make sure no one was there. When we couldn't sleep, a deputy would drive by and shine his spotlight into our home. I remember lying there on the foldout couch with my kids beside me watching that spotlight trace the ceiling of my living room until my kids and I fell asleep, knowing someone was watching over us keeping us safe.

I later learned that my then ex-husband did drive by our house at least once when he was in town for a court appearance, which was against the rules of the order of protection. So our fears were not unfounded and we are forever grateful to the Monroe County Sheriff's Office and its deputies for being our heroes and for keeping us safe for years afterward.

It has now been six years since the attack. During that time I have changed a lot and all for the better. I became a New York State certified volunteer firefighter and served for a year and a half before my job changed, have written and published my first book of poetry, "Ten Good Things About The Rain And Other Poems," have climbed Stone Mountain in North Carolina to celebrate life and survival with my dear childhood friend Bryan Hanks, and I've even gone back to my roots, literally, and am now a brunette again after living as a blonde for nineteen years. I literally got myself back and am living my life fully and authentically.

But probably the most rewarding thing I've done personally is giving back to the officers who helped get my boys back to me safely that night. On the five year anniversary, I donated three Eastern Redbud trees to the Monroe County Sheriff's Office. I chose three trees to symbolize the lives the deputies helped save that night. I chose the Redbud because its leaves are heart-shaped and its flowers are this purply pink, the color of domestic violence awareness. My boys got to meet their heroes from that night and thank them and hug them. I made a homemade meal of spinach lasagna for all of the twenty-nine deputies involved in our case and I wrote a poem for them and read it to them. Here is the text of the poem:

The Team In Blue

I thought I was in this all alone
Because no one came to help me
The neighbors went in and shut the door
So I had to play the cards dealt to me

But this was certainly not a game
My life was teetering on the bridge
Between being and not being

My fate was hanging by a smidge

His roar was like a battle cannon
Firing threats out over the lawns
Wafting down our street of war
Warning all to be quiet little pawns

And no one called for help
No one rushed over to lend a hand
They just hung their heads to the ground
And averted their eyes around that man

It told me that I didn't matter
That this abuse wasn't really so bad
That this sort of thing was normal
Despite it being the worst I'd ever had

When I did reach out for help
I was told menacing is hard to prove
I had to get more evidence
Or in court I would certainly lose

So I kept on trying to use reason
Kept trying to reframe what it was all about
If I smiled and kept the peace I thought
I'd have more time to plan my way out

But I finally ran out of precious time
When I told him I wanted to part
He punched my face and broke my nose
Before pounding me repeatedly in the heart

He did his best to strangle me
To choke the rest of me away
But I had seen the sickness growing
Although no one else saw it my way

"Oh, he would never do anything"
Is what everyone else told me
I sounded the alarm for all to hear
But the world turned away so coldly

His threats had done their job well
"The first cop dies!" he had said
The neighbors heard him scream this aloud
And knew that meant I was already dead

And so I had to become my own protector
Had to gear up for the coming fight
Had to face my own personal demon
Who came for me angrily in the dark of night

But he hadn't planned on me being smart
No, he hadn't planned on me being tough
He thought I'd cave and just die in his hands
But he found out his grip was not enough

For years I had been a runner to catch my son
Who often runs away for no reason
I lifted weights to keep strong for his visits
To keep him home for just one more season

And so it was the love for my firstborn child
And the work I did to keep him in our home

That led me to survive the attack on my life
So that my children would not be left all alone

So I got away and ran to the house next door
And banged my blood out on their walls
I was whisked inside away from the madness
But then I heard my little boys' calls

The monster had them in his possession
And I was helpless to get them back
And that's when I learned I am not alone
The men in blue had joined my attack

They raced through the night and found my loves
They saved my sons and stopped the madness
And then they protected us for years to come
Sowing happiness in our lives to replace the sadness

Never again will I have to be my own protector
And never again will I feel alone in this world
Because I learned that the bridge of life is love
And the team in blue is love for this Southern girl

- Jerri Lynn Sparks, May 29th, 2017 (Memorial Day)

I also had a Congressional letter of commendation written by departed Congresswoman Louise Slaughter who represented our district. It was a wonderful day.

And this past year I've become a public advocate and speaker to fight for better domestic violence awareness and legislation. I was on the panel for the Annual Legislative Breakfast in Monroe County and I was one of the keynote speakers for the annual Willow Domestic Violence Center

Luncheon. I've also been appointed to the Domestic Violence Consortium of Monroe County and shared my poetry and photos for the annual Art Show on the national Domestic Violence Awareness Day in April. Resolve invited me to speak at their Consortium in the spring which was the first time I'd ever spoken publicly about my ordeal. From that empowering moment much advocacy has evolved so that I am now partnering with Resolve and Willow to train first responders in domestic violence response protocols. We have trained several area fire departments and have plans to continue this critical work. I've also been invited to help advise a Congressional candidate in New York, my friend Joe Morelle, on the Violence Against Women Act and other women's health initiatives. So I've turned something horrible into positive things for my community, a full circle to the dreams I had when I was a little girl who loved politics and its possibilities.

Along the way I've made beloved friends in my fellow warriors for good, including but not limited to Jaime Saunders of The United Way (former CEO of Willow Domestic Violence Center of Greater Rochester), Allison O'Malley, founder and CEO of Resolve, Janet Chaize, my former counselor at Willow, Mary DeLella, who was my advocate at the Monroe Sheriff's Office and who attended every court session with me, my D.A. Bill Gargan, who is the best in every single way, my fellow firefighters (especially Greg Harmer who was the one who helped us get to a safe house that night), my neighbors The Brosius family (who put themselves in harm's way to shelter us), and Bob Murphy and all the other Monroe County Sheriff's Deputies who saved my boys and who have kept us safe ever since.

I also learned I have wonderful, lifelong friends and family who love us so much, including but not limited to my cousin Sharon Collins Presnell, my dear friends Alex Zapesochny and Jay Baker, who are the best bosses ever, my dear friends Jack and Verna Linney, my lifelong friend Robert Bowman and my "sister" Donna McClean who truly changed our lives. The D'Ovidios and the Slocums let me hide out at their places so I could keep on moving night to night without even hesitating a second. The Zapesochnys offered up their home for the children and me during court appearances when we were terrified. The Chandlers gave us a much-needed vacation and brought me food in one of my safe houses to comfort me when I was all alone while my kids were in hiding out of state. Donna also gave us a few vacations so we could feel like a normal family again.

The Churchville Lion's Club and the Monroe County Sheriff's Office along with the Willow Domestic Violence Center gave us meals and gifts during the holidays, items that I would not have been able to provide due to the financial ruin I was left with.

My attorney, the unflappable Alex Korotkin, listened to me rant and cry on numerous occasions during my divorce proceedings, always calmly assuring me that the law was on my side and everything would be alright (he was right). My "soul sister" Caurie Putnam-Ferguson attended court with me so I wouldn't feel alone and she went with me to apply for my pistol permit. She and her now husband Eric visited me when others were afraid to come back to our home and they included me on their lovely wedding day, showing me that indeed a broken road can lead to a more beautiful one with someone new and better someday.

My dear friend Stacy Sofia went with me on my first wedding anniversary alone so that I could celebrate freedom. My new friend Melanie Brosius taught me how to use a Sawz-all and love it and she showed me how to fix anything in a house, girl power extraordinaire.

Finally, Arthur Minery, President of Churchville Physical Therapy, was instrumental in helping me to recover physically. He has become a good friend and I am eternally grateful to him and his staff who have always been there for me. There are others who have been instrumental in our lives, too many to count, but I intend to thank them personally if I haven't done so already. My children are all doing well. We are a happy family again, thanks to all the love from so many. Hatred and revenge never win. Love wins. Love always wins.

CHAPTER 14:
DENOUEMENT

"He spoke of very simple things – that it is right for a gull to fly, that freedom is the very nature of his being, that whatever stands against that freedom must be set aside, be it ritual or superstition or limitation in any form.

"Set aside," came a voice from the multitude, "even if it be the Law of the Flock?"

"The only true law is that which leads to freedom," Jonathan said." - From "Jonathan Livingston Seagull" by Richard Bach.

While sitting in the back of the sheriff's vehicle making my statement of all that had just happened to me the early morning of July 5th, 2012, the officer asked me if I had lost consciousness. Everything was such a blur at that moment and the adrenaline was beginning to fade in my system so that I was beginning to feel an intense amount of pain.

"I did but only for a few moments I think," I said. "I don't really know how long I was unconscious."

"That's all it takes," the officer said as he continued scribbling in his notepad. "Obstructing someone's breathing until they lose consciousness is now a felony in New York State."

Being a former Congressional staffer, I knew the power that legislation could have. When I told the officer just moments later that my husband had "messed with the wrong girl" it was legislation as a weapon to fight him and other abusers that I had in mind.

After driving myself to the hospital later the morning of the attack, something that no one should have allowed me to do because my adrenaline had faded and I became dizzy while driving, I had to stop at the physical therapist's office and get treatment for my now bleeding nose so I could continue driving to pick up my little girl and take her to the safe house where my boys were. It taught me that just because a survivor looks semi-okay, they may not be.

When I got to the hospital about thirty minutes later, my daughter now safe, I panicked in the parking lot. Every man there was the attacker. I raced inside but I had no form of identification to prove who I was. The desk attendant turned me away but a passing nurse heard me and took one look at me and ushered me back to an examining room. After determining that I had not been raped she said "Good girl but your nose is broken. Let's get you to a specialist." I refused, not realizing that if I didn't get my nose set at that moment that it would become permanently crooked. Again, that shouldn't have happened. Someone should have been with me and someone should have clearly spelled out what would happen. It would be months later (September) before I would finally find time to go see about my nose and by then it was too late. So I live with a crooked nose now that reminds me of the hit and the attack sometimes.

The next morning after the attack, in incredible pain after having slept very little all night with a flathead screwdriver gripped firmly in my hand all night, I woke up and began making a list of all the things I needed to do and all the laws that needed to be made. The list was about forty-eight items long and I felt overwhelmed by it but at each court meeting and during each emotional conversation I'd have with Bill Gargan, the D.A. in my case, I would become more and more frustrated with the limitations of the law because they denied me true freedom.

It seemed that the laws were designed to protect the abuser's rights rather than mine, the survivor (I hate the word "victim" so much, to the point that even in the sheriff's vehicle that morning on July 5th, 2012 when he referred to me as a victim I corrected him and said "I'm not a victim – I'm a survivor!" I even refused to refer to my Monroe County Sheriff's Office "Victim's" Advocate as such and call her to this day instead of my Survivor's Advocate. I get that the word "victim" is designed to elicit empathy but I felt it put me in a box I didn't want to be in, that it made me seem fragile and I was a fighter. Many fellow domestic violence survivors have told me they feel the same way as I do but a few have countered that they do feel like a victim and it is part of their healing process to refer to and think of themselves as such, some of them years or even decades later. It helps them with their own self-empathy and I'm not questioning their healing journey. But for me, I immediately rejected that term to refer to myself.).

So I began making a separate list of all the things I wanted to change in the domestic violence response system. I have connections in government and in the media from my previous career in politics and I wanted to use them for good.

Shortly after I was attacked, Governor Andrew Cuomo made bath salts in New York State illegal. The very smoke shop in Brockport that my husband bought his dangerous, mind-altering chemicals from was raided a few months after the attack and it felt like a personal victory.

A few days after the attack my neighbors and I were going through the house looking for something and discovered a wooden box filled with synthetic marijuana packets. We called 911 and the police came over and submitted it into evidence. There were so many packets I couldn't believe how long my husband had possibly been taking these powerful hallucinogens. There's no telling how it damaged his brain but it explained the heavy breathing and foam coming out of his mouth during the attack. It explained the heavy breathing and how hot he felt while splashing around in the kiddie pool on the afternoon of July 4th and why he refused to turn off the air conditioner during the police chase when my boys told him they were freezing since he had grabbed them in haste before letting them dress. It explained his dilated pupils on that February 2012 snowy night. It also showed that he had a real problem with addiction that he had successfully hidden from everyone for a long time. We also found substances hidden in the bottom of an old golf bag and more than a hundred beer bottles stashed under his desk. I had never been a snoop, had always let him have his space in his office and in his "man cave" but I often wonder if some people abuse freedom while others, like me, just want to let people live freely as long as their freedom doesn't infringe upon mine.

Other laws I wanted to see enacted had to do with the structure of the judicial system. I learned that in New York State a judge can be anyone. You don't have to have any legal education. I had thought one had to be a lawyer but it's not true. The local court in the town I live had a "judge" who set bail for my mentally deranged husband who had hours earlier tried to kill me and kidnapped my two little boys on a high-speed chase at only a few thousand dollars. This was a man who had access to money from his very educated Ivy League family and the judge set the bail at a few thousand dollars? Did he not realize the dangerousness of this domestic violence attacker? That's why the cops showed up with my boys and handed us all black trash bags and said "You've got five minutes to grab your things." They knew that at any minute the attacker could be free to come and finish the job. This was systemic madness!

It is very sad when one of the most daunting madmen you're facing is the very legal system designed to protect you. It is sickening when it protects the rights of the offenders better than it protects the injured.

So judges need to be legally trained in my opinion so that they fully understand the foundations of law, the intricacies of case history, and can mete out proper sentencing. Judges should have law degrees.

Bail should be much higher for cases of domestic violence, which is one of the most deadly types of crimes. There should also be a much longer holding period for someone with so much evidence against them, allowing the injured a chance to find safe housing and gather their things and to make arrangements for childcare and schooling.

When I had my court cases, I had to face the attacker in court. I nearly vomited from the fear of being anywhere near him again. When he entered court I held my head down and stared at the floor, refusing to let him ever look me in the eyes again. He always loved my eyes so it was my little act of defiance in denying him a chance to look me in the eyes. I didn't want to see his cold or pitiful face. I didn't want to give him a chance to convey anything to me, be it regret or threats. The last time he ever looked me in the eyes was when I was running away from him barefoot and bloodied from his blows. I should not have had to be in the same room with him ever again. There is now an option for remote testimony and I'm so thankful for this because it is so re-traumatizing for survivors to have to be in "incessant proximity" to madmen who have tried to kill them or injure them in any way.

Menacing shouldn't be so hard to prove in the eyes of the law either. This is an area of prevention we really need to work on in society and in the law. A protocol needs to be developed so that police officers and 911 operators can have a checklist to fill out. A record can be made to show a history. Responses to callers should be more comprehensive and sympathetic instead of dismissive or resigned. And verbal threats need to be kept in the Violence Against Women Act. Maybe we should rename it the Violence Against Others Act because men can be targets of domestic violence too. I know this because my three sons are survivors of domestic violence. It is terror in the home and verbal threats (a better description than verbal abuse, which many think of as merely name calling) is a form of power and control that can hinder reports to law enforcement, thus failing to create a history of 911 calls.

Instead of so many people telling me "menacing is hard to prove," which kept me in a dangerous situation far longer than it should have, a public education campaign should be built up around changes in the law. We need to educate our youth early on in kindergarten or even earlier about how to lose something with grace, how to fail and how to move on, how to choose better actions than violence. A cultural change has to accompany a legal system change.

Any public education has to be ongoing, repeated and early. It has to be systemic. Firefighters, EMTs, law enforcement officers, doctors, nurses, teachers and preachers need to know what to do, what to look for and how to listen and what to ask.

Finally, money needs to be invested in safe houses with full security. Until we can reduce the numbers of domestic violence, many people are trapped tonight because they have no money and no place else to go. I was once one of them. There are seventy people awaiting placement in a shelter tonight here in Monroe County where I live. That's not even counting their children.

We have an epidemic and we're not fighting it as best we can. We have so-called zombie properties so let's flip them for good. We have commercial buildings sitting empty so let's utilize them. We have so much vacant space in this country yet we have people living in fear for their lives, women and children, and yes, some men, because we don't creatively find ways to help them.

If this book can have any positive impact in society, I hope that this message is a big part of it:

As endurers, survivors or victims of domestic violence, we did *nothing* to cause this. So many well-meaning people tell domestic violence survivors that "I hope you get counseling so that this never happens to you again," as *if* this was somehow our fault or we took actions that caused it. Look, really *look* at and scrutinize that statement and hear me, *listen* to me: Abusers OWN their abuse. Abusers are the ones *responsible* for the abuse. *Abusers* are the ones who *cause* domestic violence when they *choose* to abuse.

Abusers choose and then survivors suffer. We have one life and it is not meant for suffering…

Survivors, endurers and victims of domestic violence did not cause abuse to happen to them. Just this morning I saw that offensive statement about not letting it happen to them again on someone's social media page, which was I'm sure a kind person trying to be helpful and supportive, but what it does is guilt the survivor into thinking they did something to warrant or bring this action of abuse on them, that they "let" it happen. What it does though is it lets the perpetrator find a scintilla of justification in the implication. No. Just no, no and NO. **Abusers are the ones who cause domestic violence.**

When three women a day are pushed from the land of the living into the land of the dead in this country, we have to fight a better battle against these aggressors. It truly is terror in the home. We go across the world fighting terrorism in Iraq and Afghanistan and design the best weaponry to thwart the aggressors but we have terror right here in our own homes. We leave archaic laws or gaps in the law here in our own homeland, in our own bedrooms, letting our own citizens remain vulnerable to faulty legal weaponry. Enough. It's time to create better tools, better weapons to fight terror in the home so that we can be free.

We are human beings and it is our right to fly freely. It is the very nature of our being.

PHOTOS

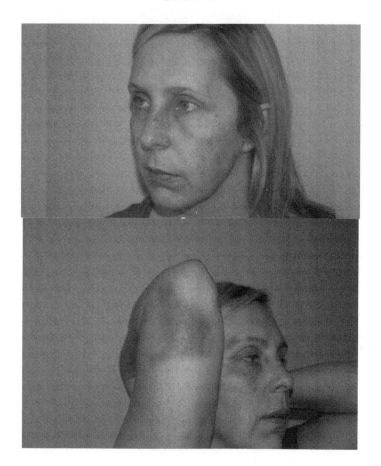

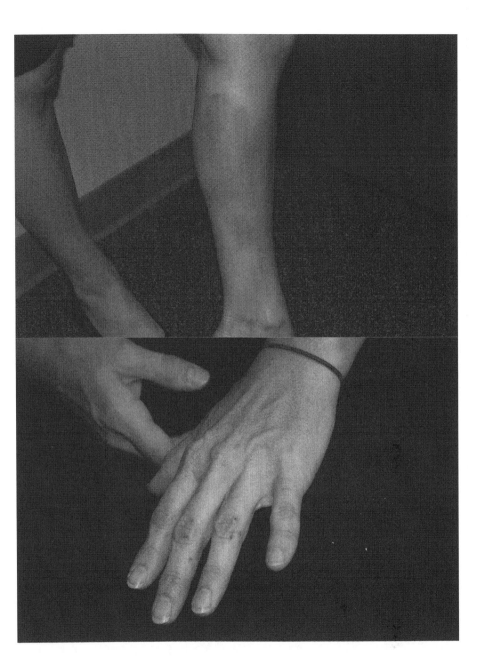

ADDENDUM

ABOUT THE AUTHOR

Jerri Lynn Sparks is a passionate advocate for the prevention of domestic violence. A former Congressional Press Secretary, she has spent most of her life advocating for better policies at the local, state and national levels. Originally from the Blue Ridge Mountains of North Carolina, she now makes her home in Western New York with her sons and a cat named Midnight who thinks he's a dog. This is her first memoir.

Thank you so much for reading one of our **Biography / Memoirs**.
If you enjoyed our book, please check out our recommended title for your
next great read!

Z.O.S. by Kay Merkel Boruff

"...dazzling in its specificity and intensity."

–C.W. Smith, author of *Understanding Women*

32837610R00084

Made in the USA
Middletown, DE
08 January 2019